C000182702

100

SUSTAINABLE

SCOTTISH

BUILDINGS

A SEDA Publication

In association with the 2016 Festival of Architecture

First Published by the Scottish Ecological Design Association 2017

With special thanks to RIAS and the 2016 Festival of Architecture.

Text and photographs have been provided by those who nominated buildings and the editorial committee. Every effort has been made to obtain copyright clearance on all images within this publication. Full acknowledgment of all contributions can be found on pp. 221-224 Please address any enquires to info@seda.uk.net

Publishing services by The Word Bank, 8 Jackson's Entry, Edinburgh EH8 3PJ

Printed in the UK by Bell & Bain Ltd, Glasgow

ISBN 978-0-9930544-5-7

A catalogue record for this book is available from the British Library

100

SUSTAINABLE

SCOTTISH

BUILDINGS

Edited by Richard Atkins and Emily Stephen

With help from Sandy Halliday, Jim Johnson, Chris Stewart and Carlos Rodriguez Campos

Architecture is at the centre of our everyday lives. It surrounds us, protects and inspires us, affects our moods, our health, our thinking. This book is not about who is 'best'; it is more important. It is a celebration of new ideas, of ingenuity, imagination, philosophy and art, a tribute to creativity, joyfulness, human scale design, an expression of our dedication to live with nature and the flow of life, to be genuinely sustainable in every possible way.

I hope this volume lands up in the libraries of every art school, school of architecture, education establishment of every kind, and on the desks of every council planning department chief, developer and every councillor in Scotland. This is not a coffee table exercise, this is an inspiration to be metaphorically inhaled for the sake of the oxygen of the ideas it contains.

My congratulations to SEDA for this magnificent gift.

Robin Harper

It is perhaps best to start with what this book is not. It is not a countdown of the top 100 most sustainable Scottish buildings ever built. It does not provide a description of how to build a sustainable building. It is not a pattern book of 'off the peg' design solutions to flick through to find the building of your choice. Depending on how you add up all the entries they possibly don't even come to 100 and arguably they are not all buildings either.

The aim of the book is to showcase the widest possible range of projects where a sustainable design approach has been adopted in response to social, economic and environmental issues. With this book we aim to illuminate the subject of sustainability as applied to the built environment.

We hope that the combination of learned essays, and the diversity of projects that can be found in just one small country, will demystify the common belief that a sustainable approach can only be delivered by narrowing the aesthetic and construction options available to the designer and client. Sustainability is a responsibility and an opportunity, not a hair shirt to be endured.

About SEDA

SEDA was formed in 1991 with the aim of sharing knowledge, skills and experience of ecological design. SEDA links those seeking information on ecological design with providers of training and practical services. There are currently around 300 members predominantly in Scotland. Members include academics, architects, artists, builders, ecologists, engineers, landscape designers, materials suppliers, planners, project managers, students, woodworkers, and many more whose work or interest is concerned with design for a sustainable future.

SEDA activities includes general networking meetings, an annual student architectural competition, tours of exemplary buildings and themed events around topics such as energy, transport, materials, building types and ecological pioneers. SEDA also co-ordinates research by its membership. Many of SEDA's members are involved in built environment issues and SEDA has researched and published building design guides – Design for Deconstruction, Design for Airtightness and Design for Toxic Chemical Reduction.

Acknowledgements

We are grateful to the Festival of Architecture for providing the funding to make this book possible, as well as to each of those who took the time to nominate a building.

We thank Richard Atkins, Chris Butters, Sandy Halliday, Ray Cole and David Cheshire for their essays and our Patron Robin Harper for his opening remarks and ongoing support.

Our utmost thanks to Chris Stewart, Jim Johnson, Sandy Halliday, Richard Atkins, Carlos Rodriguez Campos, Trisha Atkins and Emily Stephen for their tireless efforts in reviewing and editing the book and to Sean Bradley and Jennie Renton for their publishing help and guidance.

Our final thanks are to the members of SEDA who have guided the book from the outset and have provided their continued support.

Mention sustainability and you usually get one of three responses. Either your interlocutor will start foaming at the mouth saying it is all hogwash and you are a loony who wants to destroy their way of life. Or they will glaze over and look for someone else to talk to. Or if you are really lucky they will give you their description of sustainability, with which you will undoubtedly disagree.

As a concept sustainability is rather simple. There are many elements of the modern world that are pretty good, for many people and our planet. Equally there are many aspects which are iniquitous or just downright dangerous.

Consider then what might be the social, economic and environmental threats which could prevent the good things continuing to happen and what is it we need to do to change the bad stuff?

The agricultural, industrial and post industrial revolutions have brought vast benefits to many – access to clean water, abundant food, safe comfortable housing, education and medicine to name a few. This human ingenuity has been achieved by an exponential growth in the use of resources and a contingent growth in the creation of waste and pollution.

The result of mankind's success has come with a shift from a predominately agrarian society to an increasingly urban society. Urbanisation has made the built environment ubiquitous. Urbanisation breaks the direct link between environment and wellbeing and it requires the creation of new social and economic structures.

Threats to our way of life, which 100 years ago were insignificant or even nonexistent are now the subject of scientific study, resulting in calls that intervention is required on a global scale. Rolling back industrialisation and urbanisation is not necessarily possible nor desirable. What we must do is devise sustainable ways of preserving the benefits of the modern world, while dealing with the unintended, and undesirable, consequences of the way in which society is ordered.

Each of the projects in this book seeks to respond to one or more of these unintended consequences. Whether that is by reducing dependence on nonrenewable resources, minimising building toxicity, acting as a catalyst for economic development, or responding to a gap in social provision.

In selecting these projects we knew it was impossible for every project to have ticked every box. We have selected projects that illustrate specific issues and we have selected projects that represent as wide a group of building types, ages, locations, construction, aesthetics and procurement processes as possible. In doing so we had to overlook projects which had a rightful claim for inclusion. Where we had a group of projects which were of roughly equal merit we tended to opt for the earliest example in recognition of their trail blazing nature.

We have categorised the projects by use, fully aware that some maybe open to the criticism that they are not replicable in the mainstream, but they deserve inclusion as examples of projects which make an attempt to address the fundamental issues that we are faced with.

Between the projects we have included 5 short essays, which cover the limits imposed by our planet and the need for buildings to be regenerative. They remind us that buildings only exist because of the need we have for shelter and that it is people and communities that are important. Finally the idea of a circular economy which retains, as far as possible, physical resources in use rather than burying them in holes in the ground shows that there are better ways of using our planets resources.

Richard Atkins

BIOSPHERIC BOUNDARIES

RICHARD ATKINS

The inventiveness of humanity has propelled us into a unique position on our planet, one where we have been able to manipulate the environment and take advantage of the resources around us to extend or improve our knowledge, lifespan, health and consequently population. The impact of this has, however, taken us beyond the limits of what the earth's biosphere can sustain long term, given our current, profligate and unintelligent use of resources.

Humanity needs to become more socially and economically inventive in order to be able to sustain cleaner and more resource efficient ways of delivering the length and quality of life we have come to expect as both a right for ourselves and for our descendants.

The debate about sustainability has, however, become hopelessly muddled. The term itself no longer has a clear and unambiguous meaning. As a result the two main goals which have emerged at a geopolitical level – that gross domestic product (GDP) per capita must continue to increase, year on year, and that we must simultaneously address climate change and its link to anthropogenic greenhouse gas emissions – have been melded together and an expectation has been placed in humanity's inventiveness to deliver new, clean, technologies. Technologies which will solve the supply side of the equation, allowing us in the meantime to ignoring the demand side.

New technologies have a place, but they generally don't displace old dirty technologies, which continue to remain in use across the majority of the globe and these new technologies can oftentimes prove, like nuclear power, to be less clean and much more expensive than they first promised.

Pause for thought. In the last century the human population quadrupled, the proportion of those living in urban areas grew from an eighth to a half, primary energy production increased tenfold and the annual extraction rate of construction ores grew by a factor of nearly forty. It is not possible for humanity to continue to use the planet's natural resources at these accelerating rates, without accepting that at some point in the foreseeable future, dramatic and so far unplanned changes will occur.

In the absence of natural boundaries, which would otherwise moderate our behaviour, we need to set and respect our own, social, economic and environmental boundaries. If we don't, we are in danger of reaching one or other tipping point where Spaceship Earth, as described by Buckminster Fuller, changes so dramatically that humanity is endangered.

Science tells us that when resources are expended, systems collapse. Post collapse new systems will emerge, but they may not include us. It is in our best interests that our planet remains stable and sustainable. Yet detrimental impacts on our own wellbeing and the environment around us are increasingly a result of human activity.

With our intellectual advantage comes a responsibility to address this risk, both for ourselves and for those other species who not only live alongside us, but on whom we rely for food, for the materials with which we build and, at a microbial level, for dealing with the waste streams we create. It is a responsibility that we have borne too lightly.

Buildings, the subject of this book, require considerable economic and environmental resources to build, use and demolish. They determine where and to a large extent how we live, work, learn and socialise. We can all identify buildings, places and communities where we would like to be, the ones which deliver those positive social and economic benefits which we aspire to. Equally we can identify the reverse and we go to considerable lengths to avoid them.

If got right, the built environment is an agent for positive change. New methodologies and mechanisms are, however, needed to ensure that the social, economic and environmental investment associated with improving and adding to the built environment delivers positive change.

If buildings continue to be procured on a minimal first cost basis, then this leaves the rest of society to cope with the externalised social and environmental costs – health, crime, waste, pollution, disaffection – associated with an underperforming, unsustainable built environment.

We need a more holistic understanding of the impacts of what we build. It is no longer sufficient to merely require that a selective few attributes, such as energy consumption and GHG emissions, are made a little bit better than before.

With every building project, the potential impacts should be assessed against the performance that the built environment as a whole must deliver to sustain a fair and just society within a stable and healthy ecological environment. It requires a greater emphasis on renewable resources, not just those of energy and raw materials, but physical and intellectual labour as well. Such an approach puts a greater emphasis on retaining and improving existing buildings and less emphasis on continuing to add more floor space, whilst at the same time still allowing existing buildings to perform badly. It places an emphasis on economic growth through qualitative improvement rather than quantitative expansion.

Such thinking presents a major challenge to existing social and economic systems, but it is an intellectual challenge well within the capabilities of humanity to meet.

Richard Atkins

HOUSES

LOTTE GLOB HOUSE & STUDIO
LOCH ERIBOLL, DURNESS

GOKAY DEVCI

In 2001, Lotte Glob, a Danish ceramic artist whose practice is closely identified with the wilderness landscape in North West Scotland commissioned a new living and working space that would enable her to integrate her practice, her business and her lifestyle. She stipulated that the design should be affordable and context sensitive, as well as complementing her aesthetic vision, reflecting her passion for the light across the hills of Sutherland. The 110m² dwelling comprises a large multipurpose double height living/sleeping/ eating space, oriented towards the South which can also be used for exhibitions, together with a compact service space to the North.

The construction is a timber post and beam structure, sitting lightly on the earth, with a linear plan and a curved roof clad with patinated copper sheets. The external walls are clad with untreated Scottish Oak shiplap boarding designed to silver with age. The East and West elevations use narrow, linear and pocket windows aligned to the sunrise and sunset.

The South elevation is fully glazed with a timber deck projecting out into the air directly towards Ben Hope across Loch Eriboll.

On completion of the house, Lotte commissioned the design of a studio where she could work, which adheres to the same principles of affordability and sensitivity to both landscape and her aesthetic vision. The studio is embedded within the contours of the landscape, reflecting the local vernacular architecture in Sutherland, such as traditional croft buildings and agricultural sheds, which all settle into the landscape with harmony.

Roofed with rust coloured corrugated iron and finished internally with local Pine boarding, the external construction is blockwork faced with reclaimed stone. The internal structure is insulated timber framing, finished with plywood. Two wing walls at West and East create a frame for an evolving sculpture garden, sited between the studio and Loch Eriboll.

Both designs incorporate local materials wrought by a local workforce. Materials were chosen that would weather in colour and texture, ageing gracefully in harmony with changes in the seasons.

PLUMMERSWOOD
RIVER TWEED

GAIA ARCHITECTS

Gaia Architects were commissioned to design a house overlooking the River Tweed. Gaia aimed to maintain its reputation for innovation and push the boundaries of sustainable housing by pioneering an exemplar passive eco house and contribute to knowledge in the important developing area of passive design, ventilation and building health. The house combines the internationally recognised Passivhaus Standard specification with Gaia's integral and groundbreaking approach to a healthy indoor climate. This places the project at the forefront of examining and optimising passive design.

Plummerswood is designed on ecological design principles and addresses resource effectiveness, toxicity cycles, indoor climate, human factors in environmental control, sustainable forestry and place making. It is the first house to be constructed in Scotland to the Passivhaus Standard using an innovative off site glueless mass timber technique known as Brettstapel. The use of Brettstapel in Scotland has its roots in a research project that investigated the potential to add value to timber in rural communities in the European Northern periphery. This encouraged an initiative by Gaia (2002) to promote UK manufacture of Brettstapel and led to the design of Acharacle School and Plummerswood.

Designing to achieve Passivhaus certification required Mechanical Ventilation Heat Recovery (MVHR), but the aim at the outset was to experiment to compare performance under mechanical and natural ventilation in this climate. The building performed extremely well in relation to energy, comfort and indoor environmental requirements. In MVHR mode the major energy uses were fan power and frost protection and so the house proved to be just as efficient in natural ventilation mode.

Gaia has a long history of involvement in healthy indoor climate, optimised material specification, ventilation and moisture management at all stages of the innovation life cycle. All the building materials were vetted against Gaia's strict non toxic and hygroscopic standards. Special attention was paid to the avoidance of synthetic and heavily processed materials and those with polluting impacts on indoor climate and on waste streams. The insulation is made from low grade wood fibres bonded by tree resin and the building fabric is vapour permeable.

Much of the internal finish is comprised of untreated timber, which offers a large hygroscopic surface area. Areas of the house that could be subjected to high levels of indoor moisture, e.g. bathrooms, kitchen and wet room, have clay board and clay plaster ceilings.

The 346m^2 house was completed in autumn 2011 and won the Scottish Homes Award for Architectural Excellence (small projects) in 2012 and a Scottish Borders Council Award.

TIMBER HOUSE
SCOTLAND'S HOUSING EXPO. INVERNESS

JOHN GILBERT ARCHITECTS

Timber House is one of the winning entries for Scotland's Housing Expo 2010. Timber House is, in fact, 2 semi-detached houses clad in corrugated aluminium, evoking traditional Highland design but constructed with cross-laminated timber (CLT).

CLT walls are made from pieces of Spruce and Pine laid together across one another and bonded to form a very strong 95mm thick panel. The prefabricated panels can be erected in a few days. As timber grows, it consumes carbon which is then locked in for the lifespan of the building. The CLT came from Sweden but the project aimed to foster a market in this type of construction, as it could easily be manufactured in Scotland using homegrown timber. This would benefit the forestry industry and wider rural economy in Scotland.

Large South facing windows to the rear face onto the gardens and make the best use of natural light and gain heat from the sun. The North facing front has smaller windows to reduce heat loss. The house has 200mm thick wood fibre insulation fixed on the outside. CLT construction makes it easier to reduce draughts through high levels of airtightness and the roof is made from prefabricated panels filled with recycled paper insulation. Timber is both warm to the touch and has high thermal mass – the ability to retain heat – which reduces temperature swings in the house and improves comfort levels.

The n-SIP panels, manufactured using Scottish grown Sitka Spruce and natural cellulose insulation, create a highly insulated, comfortable internal environment. The panels include Oriented Strand Board manufactured near Inverness from Highland grown timber.

TWO DETACHED HOUSES AT COMRIE
COMRIE, PERTHSHIRE

MAKAR

MAKAR – an architect led design and build business – was approached in 2011 by two families who had acquired adjacent sites on the outskirts of Comrie in Perthshire and wanted to jointly commission two individual, but complementary, houses for their respective needs. Whereas their accommodation requirements differed slightly, both had a desire for locally sourced, low energy, light filled homes.

The houses both have 4 bedrooms. One has a floor area of approximately 150m^2 in area and the other of 230m^2. They feature a common palette of materials with untreated durable Scottish grown Larch cladding, dark grey painted Redwood windows manufactured in the Highlands, and painted profiled fibre cement roof panels.

The houses were prefabricated in MAKAR's workshop in Inverness using its Natural-Structural Insulated Panel (n-SIP) closed panel system before being transported to site and erected. The finishing work on the houses was carried out by local, Perthshire builders and subcontractors under MAKAR's supervision.

The houses respond to the gently sloping topography, fine views and Southerly aspect of the site and are arranged to provide a landscaped communal entrance area with private and semi-private decked areas.

Both houses utilise air source heat pumps with underfloor heating and solar thermal panels to supplement the hot water supply. Wood fuel stoves were installed to supply secondary heating within living areas. The larger house also features a 4PkW array of photovoltaic panels.

Internal finishes are high quality throughout with Douglas Fir feature trusses, Oak doors, and stone and hardwood floors. The smaller house has a small external home office pod located close to it.

The houses combine a contemporary design, a timber-first design approach utilising Scotland's indigenous timber resource, sustainable construction, low carbon energy sources, and a concern about rural place making. The off-site manufacturing used in the project also exemplifies Modern Methods of Construction.

NEW ECO HOUSE
LANARK ROAD, EDINBURGH

SIMPSON & BROWN

This is a purpose built eco house for a retired client, in the grounds of their existing large Victorian villa. The topography of the local area means that there is a deficiency of accessible housing, and there is a very real demand for accessible retirement housing to meet the needs of the ageing population. From Lanark Road there is level access to many services such as shops, doctor's surgery, library, post office and bus stop.

Given the topography, the house has been designed to step down the site. However, the dwelling provides level access from street level to approx 40% of the house. Lower levels of the house are reached by steps which can accommodate a stair lift if required in the future. The house is open plan and, although small, the interconnected spaces feel much larger.

The existing house had an established garden with substantial planting and crops. The development recognised this and retained as much of the existing vegetation as possible, and will provide for new planting and vegetable plots within the newly created garden.

The house has been designed as an eco house and achieves this on many levels. It sits lightly on the site, which minimised any excavation and the need for any earth or fill materials to be brought to the site. In construction it utilised natural building materials with low embodied energy, sourced as local to the site as possible. The house is heavily insulated to minimise heat loss and is designed to benefit from passive solar gain. The minimum heat input required is provided via a Mechanical Ventilation Heat Recovery (MVHR) system.

Fenestration is minimised to the North and exploited to the South with large amounts of glazing. The building achieves good daylighting levels to minimise the requirement for artificial lighting during the day. The roof is a sedum roof, replacing the lost footprint of vegetation onto the roof. This will attenuate the rainwater collected on the roof and excess will be collected for use in the garden.

THE HOUL
RIVEN KEN VALLEY

SIMON WINSTANLEY

The house is situated in a natural concave area of hillside, principally facing West along the natural contours of the site, to enjoy the spectacular landscape setting of the River Ken valley and the ridges of the Rhinns of Kells hills opposite.

The intention was to create a contemporary single storey 'long house' which is recessive in the landscape, sustainable in its construction, with a very low energy consumption, and an aim of zero net emissions of carbon dioxide for all energy use in the house.

The design uses lightweight but highly insulated steel and timber-frame construction which is clad in Cedar weatherboarding that has been allowed to weather to a natural silver grey colour. The roof finish is pre-weathered grey standing seam zinc. Windows and external doors are triple-glazed high performance timber, painted grey. All insulation levels are to Passivhaus standards.

The slope of the roof of the main living accommodation follows the slope of the hillside, with the rear roof meeting the main roof at a shallower angle to allow morning sunlight to penetrate the centre of the house.

The entrance to the house is sited on the North East side of the house, under the cover of the roof to provide shelter from the prevailing wind. The principal rooms are situated along the contour of the site, to enjoy the views across the valley to the West. The ancillary spaces are generally to the rear.

The house has achieved net zero carbon by using very high levels of insulation, minimising air infiltration, being heated by an air source heat pump and ventilated with a 'whole house heat recovery ventilation system'. Electricity is generated by a wind turbine and solar photovoltaic panels.

30

MODEL D HOUSE
OLD RAYNE, INSCH, ABERDEENSHIRE

GOKAY DEVECI

Model D House demonstrates the innovative and creative use of entirely homegrown timber, costing (in 2012) less than £950 per square metre to build. The Model D House offers a viable and affordable housing option for rural communities where fuel poverty is a major concern.

This showhouse incorporated sustainability into every facet of its design, creating a solution that not only ticked the boxes of sustainability criteria, but also responds to environmental, social, cultural challenges, and the needs of the users, while still producing architecture that uplifts and inspires.

Situated near Insch in Aberdeenshire, the Model D showhouse is designed to demonstrate an alternative to the expensive and often disengaging properties offered by volume developers. The Model D house was constructed almost entirely from homegrown timber, and was designed to meet the Government's zero carbon target for new housing developments then due in 2016. It is built with an innovative double stud system for wall and roof construction which incorporates continuous use of polythene sheeting for a maximum airtightness to meet the Passivhaus

standards for airtightness. The total energy use, including space heating and all the appliances and domestic hot water, is less than 120 $kWh/m^2/$ year.

The heating requirement is reduced by means of passive measures to the point that there is no longer any need for a conventional heating system. The heating requirement for the Model D house is about 1600 kWh/ year, which is approximately a tenth of what an average 'traditional' 3 bedroom rural house uses. A solar thermal panel system by Velux system further reduces the energy bill for hot water by over 50%.

The plan layout is adaptable and the current accommodation comprises a double height open plan living, dining and kitchen area, a work space, 2/3 bedrooms, a shower room and bathroom over a 1¾ storey layout.

The development proves that sustainable and energy efficient design is possible on a low budget and that its affordability has not been achieved at the expense of architectural or construction quality.

EDENHOPE
THE SCOTTISH BORDERS

SARAH ENO & ANDY SWALES

Edenhope is a house that cost relatively little to build, costs little to live in and is consistent with key environmental aspirations.

The design solution revolved around the practical application of solar design in an essentially commoditised build. The design process was based on deciding on an energy model; energy being understood as the main cost in use, and finding the most cost effective way of realising it.

The result embodies simpler, cheaper ideas in a spacious house with all energy costs in construction and occupation covered or offset by solar gains. There are both passive and active solar thermal (innovatively internally mounted) and photovoltaic panels. The design was strongly led by this solar strategy, based on energy modelling.

The house has a hybrid electricity supply; predominately off grid, but a battery which can be charged by off peak renewable grid power in times of need. The house has passive/active performance;

the shell has good but not excessive insulation (< 0.1 W/m²K) with good quality low-e double glazing. There is a high level of airtightness in a direct passive solar design; with thermal mass provided by clay plaster, maintaining its temperature at night.

The solar thermal performance is such that the house warms up even on overcast days, with the solar gain exceeding any heat loss. A Mechanical Ventilation Heat Recovery system supplies the main spaces and is coupled to a subsoil heat exchanger. This allows the house to be ventilated with air prewarmed in winter and precooled in summer, when operating without heat recovery.

The solar thermal panel under a section of glazed roof provides hot water without added weatherproofing or frost protection equipment. Located in a warm space, it gives good year-round performance. It directly feeds a thermal store along with a back boiler in a small stove and immersion heaters powered by photovoltaic generation or cheap off-peak renewable grid electricity.

Edenhope was shortlisted for the Kerr MacGregor Memorial Award for Solar Innovation. Nominated in 2008 by longstanding member of the Scottish Solar Energy Group Paul Simpson 'for innovations in creating a self built autonomous house ... without the benefit of any formal education in engineering, architecture or building ... driven by an environmentally responsible attitude towards the planet'.

SUBURBAN PASSIVE HOUSE
NORTH BERWICK

BRENNAN & WILSON ARCHITECTS

Built to stringent Passivhaus standards, this home, located in a typical suburban street, provides a model for future living. It offers flexible family accommodation combined with thermal comfort and very low running costs.

The main living area has been designed to be adaptable: either completely open plan, or with various rooms which can be closed off to provide greater separation or privacy. The external building fabric is heavily insulated. The wall panels are formed from an innovative, but extremely simple prefabricated space stud timber frame and the roof panels are formed from timber I-joists, both almost completely eliminate thermal bridging.

The airtight construction achieved an air pressurisation test result of 0.75m^3/ m^2.hr @ 50pa, equivalent to 0.59 air changes per hour and space heating requirements are just 16kw/m^2 per annum. In the first year of occupation the house was monitored by Edinburgh University, to assess predicted energy use with actual.

The house is heated by solar gain through large South facing windows, incidental gains from appliances, lighting, towel rails and people. In colder weather, back-up is provided by a 2kw heating element in the Mechanical Ventilation Heat Recovery ventilation system. Photovoltaic panels on the roof generate 3.7PkW of electricity, with solar thermal panels, providing a significant contribution to the domestic hot water supply. LED lighting has been provided throughout.

The house was constructed from a timber frame, with insulation made from recycled materials. The concrete slab was mixed from reclaimed potash and timber flooring came from reclaimed sources. The slate worktops in the bathrooms were cut from salvaged snooker table tops. Externally the materials are a simple palette of stained Scottish timber cladding and slate on the roof. The gable walls are clad in wood fibre board finished with a lime based render.

2 SEMI-DETACHED HOUSES
LOCHCARRON, WESTER ROSS

MAKAR

The Highlands Small Communities Housing Trust (HSCHT) aims to provide affordable housing in small, rural communities across the Highlands. In recent years MAKAR has designed and delivered 13 houses for HSCHT in 5 different communities.

The house designs vary according to the topography and features of each site. Completed in 2015 the homes constructed at Lochcarron comprise 2 semi-detached blocks of 2 bedroom homes; with an area of 65m² per unit.

The site at Lochcarron was very challenging – a steep South facing slope above the main part of the village. The design makes use of the site by lifting the houses off the ground on European Larch piers.

The homes were built using MAKAR's closed system to form wall, floor and roof assemblies; Natural-

Structural Insulated Panel (n-SIP). The panels were manufactured using Scottish grown Sitka Spruce and cellulose insulation. Cladding is Highland grown untreated European Larch.

Each home has a very low embodied carbon content because of the timber first and local sourcing philosophies that were used to guide the design and construction.

A key feature of the houses are large South facing windows in the living areas that give extensive views out over Loch Carron.

The units were manufactured off-site and exemplify a Modern Methods of Construction approach to the delivery of sustainable, low carbon homes in rural Scotland.

KINCRAIG MILEHOUSE
CAIRNGORMS NATIONAL PARK

DAVID SOMERVILLE ARCHITECTS

Four new affordable houses were completed for the Highland Small Communities Housing Trust as part of their aim to provide affordable and sustainable housing in the countryside. The objective was to minimise the physical impact of the development process, whilst maximising the opportunity for the occupants.

Built from timber-framed panels constructed off-site, to give greater quality control, with foundations designed to minimise physical impact on the ground. The foundations were formed in concrete pipes which support and hold down the building. An arrangement which can be replicated on sites with difficult ground conditions and which might otherwise be dismissed as undevelopable.

The landscaping has been carefully considered and the minimum numbers of trees were felled to maintain a forest setting. The 4 houses are set out in plots in excess of half an acre, much bigger than sites normally associated with affordable housing. The large size of plots allows the possible development of home based work initiatives. The system of financing has made it possible to provide family houses at a reasonable cost to local people. The construction cost of £140,000 per house would not normally be sufficient to buy a house site of this size in this area. The houses have several key features:

- Very high insulation values; 300mm of insulation in walls, roof and floor, giving a heat load for the house of 5kw at 10 deg below zero with inside temperature of 21 deg.
- Low carbon emissions $6.94 kg/m^2/year$ – EI rating 94 EI band A.
- A woodburning stove which heats most of the house, dispersing heat by natural convection through the open plan living areas. The stove has a boiler linked to a 210 litre thermal store. This store serves domestic hot water and radiators in areas not served by natural convection.
- Renewable energy integrated into the heating system – $4m^2$ solar thermal panels are linked to the thermal store and provide a significant contribution to heat supply, mainly in the summer months when the stove is less likely to be in use.
- The houses are constructed, as much as is possible, using locally sourced materials and expertise, benefiting the local economy and reducing the transport costs.

TRESSOUR WOOD
WEEM, PERTHSHIRE

GAIA ARCHITECTS

The house pioneered Gaia's use of 'breathing' or moisture transfusive construction in Scotland, along with numerous other aspects of ecological construction. Following a change of site, the house was approved as it was perceived as being 'in a wooded environment'.

The house has high levels of cellulose fibre insulation and benign structural and finishing materials. None of the timber was chemically treated, either internally or externally, and all wall, floor and ceiling finishes are natural and non toxic.

It is heated by a combination of passive solar gain and a woodburning stove. The open plan allows for the heat to rise up through the solar staircase atrium which has magnificent views over the Perthshire countryside. Summer cooling is achieved via stack effect through the same atrium, with a vent at the roof apex.

The exemplary design has been much copied, albeit not always well, and even claimed by others. It has taken its rightful place as a classic of modern design, as well as a forerunner of high quality sustainable rural housing.

The project won UK House of the Year in 1993.

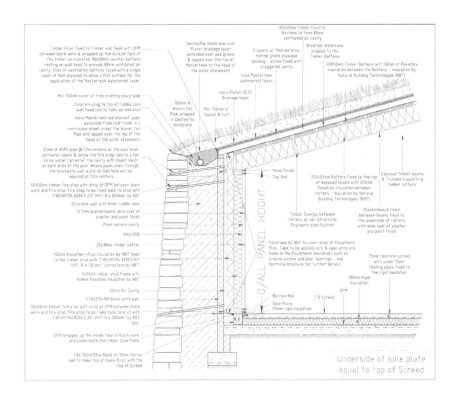

THE STONEHOUSES
ULLAPOOL, WESTER ROSS

SBA ARCHITECTS

SBA were commissioned to design 2 luxurious holiday cottages which would provide 5 Star holiday accommodation, maximising the views and enhancing the chosen site. The cottages were to be as ecologically sound as economically viable.

The site has a spectacular outlook but is exceedingly steep with a 1 in 2.5 gradient and it was overgrown by rhododendron. The self build clients persevered to clear the site and the design was then completed to exploit both views and topography.

A further practical difficulty lay in the shared ownership of an access road which required to be improved and surfaced causing both delays and additional costs to the project.

A temporary vehicular works access was built, but only the most experienced 4-wheel drivers, quads or tracked vehicles could manage it. This meant that a lot of materials had to be hauled up the hill by hand, making this a very difficult project to complete.

The very intrepid and determined clients with a team of local crafts people and artisans were brought together by the traditional building techniques and the modern design and environmental consideration to ensure that the cottages were finished to the high standard required.

Sustainable technologies were incorporated, with solar thermal panels providing hot water and an air source heat pump providing underfloor heating. The cottages now nestled into a hillside above the beautiful village of Ullapool – two 5 Star holiday retreats built from stone, turf and glass.

A tremendous amount of care was taken to ensure that both the exteriors and interiors of the buildings sit comfortably in the local landscape and are suitably fitting for the site.

JAPANESE HOUSE
EDINBURGH

KONISHI GAFFNEY ARCHITECTS

In 2009 Konishi Gaffney Architects completed their own self build house and studio in Edinburgh. In 2010 it won the 'Best Small Project' award from the Edinburgh Architecture Association.

It is built on a small brownfield site, formerly a mechanic's garage, on a back lane. This congested and overlooked site required a careful balance between privacy and maximising the benefits of both sunshine and solar access. It succeeds by turning its back on the lane to protect privacy, while to the East, a 5.5m x 2.4m opening to the garden allows the early morning sun in, starting the heating cycle. To the South, a large glazed 1st floor corner window brings light and warmth diagonally through a double height space onto the thermal mass of a solid floor.

Passive solar techniques and local, recycled and recyclable materials were specified throughout and the house is super insulated. The result is that in spring, summer and autumn, while the sun is high enough, the house requires no heating. In winter, underfloor heating provides comfortable and efficient space heating and top-up heating is provided by a woodburning stove.

The house was designed whilst living and working in Japan (2007) and as a Scottish-Japanese practice a number of Japanese themes were adopted. Local materials were selected throughout; the Scottish Oak used for cladding, balustrades, raised dado rails and sliding glass doors all came from two small hardwood timber mills less than 20 miles away.

SIGNAL STATION HOUSE
NORTH QUEENSFERRY, FIFE

ICOSIS ARCHITECTS

This Signal Tower is a Category B listed ex-Ministry of Defence structure overlooking the Firth of Forth and was purchased by the clients in 2001. The brief was to renovate the existing tower and add a large modern extension, using environmentally sustainable materials and methods, in order to create a contemporary family house.

The orientation and positioning of the new building responds to the exposed coastal location of the site, the views and the movement of the sun, whilst also maximising the remaining garden area. The predominantly solid East and West walls are bookends sandwiching an all glass South elevation, which frames the garden and the Forth Rail Bridge and optimises solar gain. Rooflights above the corridor spine of the new structure allow natural light to penetrate to the heart of the building.

In Phase 1, the signal tower was stripped back internally to its original brick walls and concrete floors, a new timber staircase was installed and the walls were lined using sheep's wool insulation and clay boards, with a clay plaster finish. The existing windows were replaced with triple-glazed timber units and the flat concrete roof was insulated above

with cork and sealed using EPDM rubber membrane.

In Phase 2, the extension was built using pre-manufactured timber cassettes insulated with cellulose insulation, erected in three days onto a pre-prepared base. The main walls are a hygroscopic construction with untreated Scottish Larch cladding and woodwool slabs, finished with a lime render. The recycled elements were each whitewashed using a water based mineral paint, in order to match the aesthetics of the original tower and unify the whole. The planted turf roof on the extension, uses the soil from the foundations, which was kept aside and reinstalled upon completion. The roof is viewed from the Forth Rail Bridge above and the turf helped to minimise the visual impact of the extension whilst introducing a high level of acoustic insulation to the house.

A construction phase waste management strategy was implemented to minimise the need for transporting waste to landfill over the course of the project; all untreated timber waste was retained for use in the two woodburning stoves, whilst the brick and rubble from Phase 1 were used as fill and sub-base beneath the extension.

Ellieside Cottage received an award from the Association for the Protection of Rural Scotland in 2000 and was included in the 2001 Scottish Executive good practice guide on sustainability.

ELLIESIDE COTTAGE
CULLEN

NICK BROWN PLANNING

Ellieside Cottage was built on the edge of the Cullen policies in 1825 by the Earl of Seafield and it is thought to have been a Farm Manager's cottage until becoming vacant around 1960. It was bought from the Estate in 1990 as a 'building plot', due to the state of dereliction and was restored and extended between 1994 and 1999.

The cottage was restored using recycled materials including salvage from the existing ruin, old pantiles, roof timbers, flagstones and lintels from various derelict buildings on the Estate, sanitary-ware from a fire damaged house in Cullen and flooring from a manse in Fochabers. Radiators from Dr Gray's Hospital and worktops from a demolished science lab in Aberdeen were also recycled and reused. The porch and the rear link were rebuilt in breathing wall construction and are sympathetic to the original house.

The extension copies the footprint of the original house, but is clearly different and is the result of consultation with neighbours, Planners and Building Control. Card models were used in the consultation to help others visualise the new extension. The family room extension is inspired by Nissen huts and railway carriages, frequently found in rural North East Scotland. The extension was constructed using timber I-columns and timber panels, and the building is clad in zinc.

Organic internal paints were used throughout the project, including lime mortar and limewash finishes over stone and Keim mineral paint over render. Central heating and hot water are provided by a biomass boiler with photovoltaic solar panels linked to an emersion heater. Space heating is provided by two solid fuel burners, using logs harvested from the site. Passive stack ventilation takes solar gain to the upper level and rainwater drains to the nearby duck pond.

A pantile and timber shed, formally a cow shed, has been rebuilt to match the description of neighbours, including a brick floor salvaged from a derelict brickworks and reintroducing the apex opening to encourage nesting swallows.

This year the cottage has had over 23 different species of bird nesting in the garden, as well as a colony of bats in the carport roof.

MAINS OF BRANSHOGLE
STIRLINGSHIRE

SIMPSON & BROWN

Two farm cottages at Mains of Branshogle in Stirlingshire were extended and remodelled to form a single home. The project demonstrates the commitment of one individual to produce a building that can be used as a learning tool for others, despite cost and builder constraints.

The design was driven by a desire to build with natural, traditional and local materials, and to have systems in place that could be manually controlled; a low-tech approach to sustainability, rather than relying on automated systems, was adopted. The project provided a valuable opportunity to explore various construction methods and materials in innovative ways.

The house takes advantage of passive solar gains and uses the massive stone external walls as a heat sink with a sun porch running the entire length of the South elevation. The thermal mass potential of the existing perimeter walls was exploited by insulating the masonry on the outside face, using sheep's wool quilt overlaid with reed lath and finished with soft lime plaster, thereby retaining internally generated heat inside the building fabric.

A new extension has been constructed on the footprint of a derelict barn, which was a source of salvaged stone to create the plinth courses of the new structure.

The main frame of the extension is a pegged green Oak assembly using locally felled timbers, infilled with a breathing wall construction made up of heavily insulated timber panels. This was externally clad with untreated larch boarding and lined internally with unfired clay bricks. This reverses the conventional timber frame construction creating more thermal mass on the inside of the structure.

Solar thermal panels and a woodburning stove provide heat to the underfloor and radiator heating systems and passive solar gain has been maximised throughout. The whole house is naturally ventilated.

With the help of volunteers, a straw bale donkey house and garage were also constructed. These were finished with lime harling and limewash to match the main house, and a sedum blanket roof to marry it to the landscape.

REFURBISHMENT OF 11 ANNAT ROAD
PERTH

HISTORIC SCOTLAND

This sandstone cottage was built in 1927 as part of a new development of rented housing on the edge of Perth by the local businessman and philanthropist Arthur Kinmond Bell. The houses were designed to a high standard; the habitable area is 78m². Perceptions of health, environment and buildings were given high importance by AK Bell, and instructions as to the appropriate levels of ventilation were fixed onto the wall of each house. This property, and 146 others of similar configuration close by, have been operated as affordable housing, with market rents, for many years by the Gannochy Trust, which was established by AK Bell in 1937.

Some previous fabric upgrades had resulted, however, in poor internal conditions and detrimental effects on the building fabric. As a result the Trust decided to review the upgrade works and implement a more sympathetic approach to refurbishment. Working with Historic Environment Scotland a revised template of upgrades was developed which did not just focus on low U-values for building components, but ensured appropriate ventilation for the building occupants and fabric. The original character of the buildings and the internal finishes were considered important and contributed to occupant wellbeing at a number of levels. In contrast to previous refurbishments, internal fittings were repaired and retained.

The works were delivered by the Trust's Estate Management Staff and local contractors. While many of the techniques were new, they were quickly learnt and overall refurbishment costs were lower than the more standard and invasive techniques previously used. The stone walls were insulated by the application of a water based foam behind the existing lath and plaster linings; and in situ measurement of U-Values have indicated a reduction from 0.98 to 0.41 W/m²K while maintaining acceptable levels of relative humidity within the core of the wall. Other measures were wood fibreboard insulation to the floors and roof space. Blocked flues were partially reopened to allow a degree of modest background ventilation. These and other measures are described in detail in Historic Environment Scotland's Refurbishment Case Study 20.

The works were carried out over autumn of 2014 and the property has been occupied by tenants since March 2015. A project outcomes review in 2017 will establish in more detail the energy saved as a result of the works.

SCOTSTARVIT TOWER COTTAGE
CUPAR, FIFE

HISTORIC ENVIRONMENT SCOTLAND & THE NATIONAL TRUST FOR SCOTLAND

Nestled behind a bank of trees down a quiet lane in rural Fife, Scotstarvit Cottage is a detached 19th century cottage, near the bustling village of Cupar and has been little altered since its construction. It retains the original sash and case windows, lath and plaster finishes, decorative cornicing and fireplaces. With mass masonry and lime-mortared walls, suspended timber floors and a pitched slate roof, in construction, it is similar to thousands of properties across Scotland.

Prior to refurbishment the property was cold, draughty and poorly insulated, making it inefficient to heat and keep warm. In 2012, it was identified as being suitable for a 'whole-house' sustainable refurbishment, demonstrating how traditional, and even historically sensitive, buildings can be upgraded to modern energy efficiency standards. The refurbishment philosophy of the project team was conservation driven, with an approach of minimal intervention and protection of historic features. Site waste was to be minimised. The specification for refurbishment was based on natural, breathable materials, to ensure compatibility with the building's existing construction and reduce impact on the environment during the building's lifecycle.

Emphasis was placed on making the building healthy for occupants, ensuring adequate ventilation, heating, and minimising indoor pollutants. Hemp insulation was installed beneath the existing timber floor and in the attic. Secondary glazing was fitted and the walls were insulated with breathable perlite insulation. The perlite insulation was poured behind the original lath and plaster linings, which remained undisturbed. The old oil-fired boiler and wet central heating were replaced with high efficiency electric infra red panels – economical to run and beneficial to health. Natural clay paint was used for redecoration to complete the project.

The refurbishment allowed all the original features to be retained, conserving the building's historic character, whilst increasing thermal efficiency. Individual elements were significantly improved, raising the EPC rating from F to D. Airtightness tests met current building standards, whilst passive ventilation was retained to provide a healthy indoor environment. The improvement of insulation to the timber suspended floor resulted in this element exceeding current building regulations for thermal efficiency.

Scotstarvit Cottage is now a thermally efficient and environmentally sustainable traditional building, retaining all its original charm. It is currently let to a long-term tenant.

THE RINGS
RING FAR, CHANCE INN, CUPAR, FIFE

CHAMBERS MCMILLAN

The Rings are 2 wheelchair accessible holiday cottages, inspired by the client's family experience of not being able to go on holiday as wheelchair users. The client was granted permission to build on the green belt as the cottages were part of a farm diversification project and received an ERDF funding grant for around one third of the costs.

The cottages provide inclusive and accessible accommodation that feels spacious and light. The site is in the green belt of Fife, on a steep rolling hill. The building is integrated into the landscape by creating 2 folding sedum roofs: in plan a wedge like form minimises the impact from the village road and allows more accommodation on the South facing side taking advantage of the views. By moving to a compact single storey form, the cottages are completely accessible, and this kept the ridge line lower, allowing an unbroken view of the horizon from the road, which was a key planning concern.

The cottages offer wheelchair users and their families and friends the opportunity to go on holiday in an accessible building, which doesn't have the aesthetic of an institutional building.

The cottages' flexibility allows for many variations of use: from booking both cottages for 16 people, to one apartment for two. This provides an inclusive sustainability. Spaces connect directly to the surrounding countryside, both visually and physically, enhancing the spatial experience and providing freedom of movement for those using wheelchairs.

The cottages have an air source heat pump combined with a hybrid LPG boiler, and each cottage has a 4PkW photovoltaic panel array. Externally one cottage is clad in Cedar shingles and the other in vertical Scottish Larch. Carved out from these building forms are small covered external spaces and each of the bedrooms has direct access to the outside. The inclusive and flexible design, informed by its context, gives these cottages a long-term sustainability by providing spaces that are not usually provided, but are greatly needed.

THE RAMP HOUSE
PORTOBELLO, EDINBURGH

CHAMBERS MCMILLAN

The Ramp House is an inclusive lifetime home which is sustainable both in its built fabric and in a wider conceptual sense. A building which is flexible and inclusive, so that it can continue to be used as people's needs change, ensures that its usefulness and lifespan is maximised.

Self commissioned as a family home, the brief included the needs of Greta, who has impaired mobility. Ramps provides access and an equality of space to all of the family, linking spaces together. Sitting in the living room, Greta can see, hear and communicate with family and friends in 6 other spaces.

The Ramp House provides spaces which enable Greta's development, changing needs and provides a sustainable, long-term, lifetime environment.

The process of building the Ramp House became a vehicle through which the local community could include themselves, support the family and demonstrate the extent to which they valued the project of inclusivity. This enables Greta to remain in the heart of her community and this accessible family home allows her and her friends to come and play just like any other youngsters.

The Ramp House is inclusive in the way that it is used, it challenges and transforms perceptions and assumptions of disability. By putting Greta at the centre of the space, the 'levelling' that is experienced, both by Greta and by visitors, suggests a way of designing, building and living where disability is not 'different'.

The Ramp House provokes a wider societal debate and demonstrates that sustainability requires equality of accessibility and a socially inclusive approach to the built environment.

HOUSING

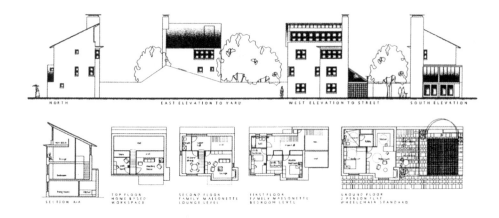

HOMES FOR THE FUTURE
GLASGOW GREEN, GLASGOW

AUSTIN-SMITH: LORD

As part of Glasgow's City of Architecture celebrations in 1999, Austin-Smith: Lord (ASL) were asked to take part in this groundbreaking scheme to design 'Homes for the Future'. The aim was to provide small affordable homes which were flexible in arrangement, barrier free and low in energy consumption.

These two homes are on a narrow city centre site, each with its own conservatory / entrance space. Both homes are highly insulated, with a SAP rating of 100. ASL worked with a local housing developer to create a prototype three storey building that drew on Scottish vernacular architecture but also placed emphasis on energy conservation and access for wheelchair users.

The ground floor apartment is designed to suit wheelchair users while the upper maisonette is designed to be barrier free and suit a family with a need for home based workspace. The building was designed to catch and conserve solar energy through the inclusion of buffer spaces at the entrances, the use of natural daylight into all rooms and by incorporating photovoltaic tiles into the roof finish.

The very steeply roof profile helps to deflect wind and provide shelter to the public side of the building. This also helps to reduce heat loss due to wind exposure.

The building fabric used recycled aggregate blockwork, sustainable timber and very high levels of insulation. Low energy light fittings, a high efficiency woodburning boiler, low water usage toilets and tap fittings were also used.

The influence of this project can be found in Austin-Smith: Lord's subsequent projects, which incorporate many of the same design principles,along with increased thermal performance of the building envelope.

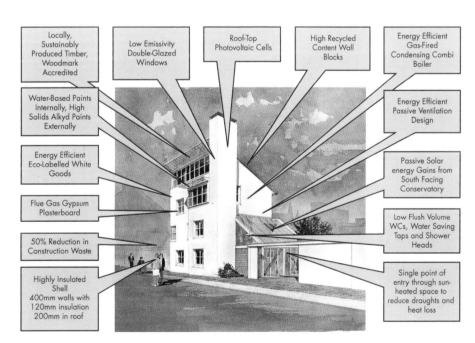

Locally, Sustainably Produced Timber, Woodmark Accredited

Low Emissivity Double-Glazed Windows

Roof-Top Photovoltaic Cells

High Recycled Content Wall Blocks

Energy Efficient Gas-Fired Condensing Combi Boiler

Water-Based Paints Internally, High Solids Alkyd Paints Externally

Energy Efficient Passive Ventilation Design

Energy Efficient Eco-Labelled White Goods

Passive Solar energy Gains from South Facing Conservatory

Flue Gas Gypsum Plasterboard

Low Flush Volume WCs, Water Saving Taps and Shower Heads

50% Reduction in Construction Waste

Single point of entry through sun-heated space to reduce draughts and heat loss

Highly Insulated Shell 400mm walls with 120mm insulation 200mm in roof

All dwellings have sunspaces,
active solar water heating and
space for future photovoltaics.

EAST WHINS
FINDHORN, FORRES

JOHN GILBERT ARCHITECTS

Designed for and with Duneland, a social enterprise group focused on sustainability, East Whins Ecovillage is a mix of 25 homes; twelve 2 bedroom flats, ten 2 bedroom houses and three 3 bed houses – with co-housing facilities, including a large common room, kitchen and meeting room. The development incorporates a communal laundry with passive solar drying room and there are 7 'flexi-units' which enable residents to work from home. The social spaces are included to strengthen community bonds and provide the residents with the benefits of shared activities including cooking, health and wellbeing and arts & crafts.

There is no in-curtilage parking; instead cycling is promoted and a large central bike store is provided. The houses are constructed in terraces and are designed and built to a standard close to Passivhaus levels. Low energy timber windows and doors were used and thermal bridging has been eliminated.

For the floor, an insulated structural raft former wraps the whole ground floor slab in insulation, completely eliminating the thermal bridge at perimeter walls.

All dwellings have sunspaces, active solar water heating and space for future photovoltaic panels. The South facing roof pitch is designed to maximise panel efficiency at the spring and autumn equinox, when solar energy is most beneficial.

Wind turbines within the wider Findhorn community are net exporters to the National Grid, making the whole community zero carbon. East Whins is connected to the system so electric solutions which don't always make sense, do so here. Mechanical ventilation systems with heat recovery reduce the heating load and underfloor heating is fed by an air source heat pump.

THE 'TIGH-NA-CLADDACH'
(house by the shore)
DUNOON

GOKAY DEVECI

The client's aims were to develop proposals that would facilitate the provision of affordable, good quality and low energy designs of 1, 2 and 3 bedroom houses to be sold as 'Homestake' (shared equity).

The site is set against a magnificent hillside of woodland and occupies a seafront location in Dunoon that commands spectacular views of the Clyde across to Inverkip. It was sold to Fyne Initiatives by Argyll and Bute Council, on the basis that the purchaser would provide affordable housing to meet the needs of the local community, as well as leasing the woodland and providing a small workshop that would accommodate activities of the Bullwood Group.

Community participation took place in November 2008 when three design options were presented to seek local community reactions. The architectural form and proportions respect the fine tradition of Scottish vernacular architecture. They are also contemporary, and socially and culturally sustainable designs that use the best building technology available to create a sustainable way of living. The houses were designed to make a positive contribution to the built cultural heritage of the Dunoon area.

This social housing scheme was accredited by the Passivhaus Institute in 2009. The calculations based on PHPP, showed the overall energy consumption as 36.4 kWh/m²/yr, which included the space heating, domestic hot water, household and auxiliary power. The heating demand is only 15 kWh/m²/yr, a total of 1,750 kWh/yr for the whole building.

These figures prove that sustainable and energy efficient design is possible on a social housing budget. Affordability can be consistent with sustainability and it was not achieved here at the expense of architectural design or construction quality.

SLATEFORD GREEN
SLATEFORD GREEN, EDINBURGH

HACKLAND & DORE ARCHITECTS

Slateford Green is sited on a former railway goods yard in Gorgie, Edinburgh. The result of an international competition organised by the Royal Incorporation of Architects in Scotland and the Scottish Government's housing agency, the scheme comprises 120 flats and a community centre in a car free environment using energy efficient and sustainable design.

The urban block is derived from the traditional Edinburgh tenement block, with its secure sheltering courtyard form adapted to follow the topography of the site. The block is skirted by a pedestrian street and cycle route linking Gorgie and Slateford Roads, graded to provide service, drop-off and emergency access throughout.

Cycle parking is integrated into the common stair areas. Materials have been sourced for minimal environmental impact, with home grown timber studs. Ground floor units have a rainscreen of natural finished Cedar boarding, upper floor units are clad with render and the roof covering is profiled aluminium. The structure is clad with a breathing wall, comprising 170mm of cellulose insulation with Panelvent sheathing.

Heating and hot water are provided to the development by a district system powered by an on-site boiler plant using low tariff gas fuel.

A drum form roof light punctures the building at the stairwells, bringing natural light into the common areas of the building and allowing natural stack ventilation. An artificial wetland in the centre of the courtyard filters roof and road run-off following the Scottish Environment Protection Agency's water management guidelines. All areas have been planted with native, low maintenance species, chosen to encourage wildlife.

Of the flats, 26 were for sale, 25 were for shared ownership and the remaining 69 were for social rent. Four flats were specially designed for disabled tenants, and 14 flats have been adapted to provide residential and support accommodation for the Edinburgh Deaf Society.

The project was the recipient of the Chartered Institute of Housing 'Environmental Building of the Year' 1999 and the Regeneration of Scotland Award 2000 'High Commendation'.

A drum form rooflight punctures the building at the stairwells, bringing natural light into the common areas of the building and allowing for natural stack ventilation.

DORMONT ESTATE Passivhaus DEVELOPMENT
LOCKERBIE

WHITE HILL DESIGN STUDIOS

Dormont Park is an award winning rural development of 8 new 2 and 3 bedroom semi-detached Passivhaus homes. The Dormont Estate is located in Lockerbie and this multi-dwelling development achieved Passivhaus certification on completion.

Completed in 2011 and part-funded by the Scottish Government's Rural Homes For Rent pilot grant scheme, the properties are intended for long-term affordable rent. Built on a greenfield site next to an existing small building group, the new build homes have been designed to blend in with the traditional building style of the area.

The Passivhaus approach, coupled with renewable energy technology, has removed the threat of fuel poverty in the long term for the tenants of these houses. Had these houses been built to the standards required by building regulations in force at the time, it is estimated that each house would emit 63 tonnes of CO_2 every year.

By building to certified Passivhaus standards and utilising solar and biomass renewable energy, each house only emits around three tonnes of CO_2 per year – a saving of 3,600 tonnes over the projected lifespan of each house.

That also means lower energy bills in an area without mains gas, which, together with affordable rent levels, has a significant impact on tenants' disposable incomes, helping to support the survival and sustainability of a fragile rural community where the cost of goods, services and transport are higher.

GLENALMOND STREET
SHETTLESTON, GLASGOW

JOHN GILBERT ARCHITECTS

In 1998 John Gilbert Architects won this Housing Association Grant sponsored competition based on the theme of sustainable housing, creating at the time a unique project which combined solar thermal and geothermal energy to provide heating and hot water, all set within a car free environment.

There are 16 homes, providing a variety of house types and sizes designed to cater for families, young couples and the elderly. The dwellings are barrier free, as far as possible, including a ground floor WC in the terraced houses (long before these were required by regulation) and a straight stair which could accommodate a stairlift.

One of the ground floor flats is designed for wheelchair circulation. As the site is near to public transport and local shops, it was designed to be a car free scheme with only one parking bay for the wheelchair flat.

The houses are largely oriented East West, giving good daylight to back and front, with draught lobbies to reduce heat losses. They were well insulated for the time and featured one of the first uses in Scotland of recycled cellulose insulation.

The construction materials were all selected by considering their environmental impact throughout their whole lifecycle, including extraction, production, transportation, during the build, occupation and eventual demolition and decomposition.

A number of recycled materials were used. A solar ventilation system was installed in the 4 terraced houses, circulating solar pre-warmed air from the space under the roof tiles.

Air extraction in the kitchens and bathrooms is provided by a passive stack ventilation system. The housing achieves a Standard Assessment Procedure (SAP) rating in excess of 100, largely due to the use of geothermal heating.

The houses make use of geothermal energy, taking water at 12°C from a disused coal mine under the site. This water is passed through a heat pump and heats a large thermal storage tank.

The tank also receives warm water from 36m^2 of solar thermal panels. This warm water then heats the houses and provides preheated warm water as well; the running costs are in the region of £100 a year for space heating and £50 a year for hot water.

A'CHRANNAG
ROTHESAY, ISLE OF BUTE

GOKAY DEVECI

This residential tower provides 14 flats over 7 floors. The staircase and lift are located to the rear of the flats, freeing up the front to provide each living room with a balcony and a splendid view. The top floor flats have roof terraces.

The tower is one of Europe's most energy efficient social housing projects that manages to reduce the heat requirements to 1kW in each flat, thus eliminating the need for a dedicated heating system for each flat. The bedrooms do not require heating at all, and the CO_2 emission have been reduced by 70% compared to a standard build. Maximum energy efficiency was achieved by using 600mm rendered thick thermal blockwork walls with 300mm of pumped insulation, triple glazing with an airtight construction, and a Mechanical Ventilation Heat Recovery system.

Social inclusion was one of the main objectives of this scheme. In Scotland, compared with some other countries, there has traditionally been a distinct difference in appearance between public and private housing. A'Chrannag is located on the edge of town, just outside the Rothesay Conservation Area, on a brownfield site that was formerly occupied by the Foley House Hotel, demolished after a fire in 1995. The brief was to build around fourteen 2 and 3 bedroom homes for rent to meet local needs for affordable housing.

The client was Fyne Homes and they specified that the dwellings should be sustainable and innovative and that the local community should be encouraged to participate in the planning process.

Prior to the planning application, three design options were presented to the people of Rothesay; 14 detached and semi-detached houses with front and back gardens, a series of terraced blocks, and the round tower idea.

The £1.5m tower, including the site works, was built by local contractors with completion in July 2005.

e tower is one of Europe's most energy efficient social housing projects

ARCHERS HALL
BUCCLEUCH STREET, EDINBURGH

LDN ARCHITECTS

The Royal Company of Archers (RCA) in Edinburgh was founded in 1676 and is based in the 18th century Archers Hall. The brief included the replacement of the existing archery range and the design of low rise flatted accommodation for 75 University of Edinburgh students. The RCA's long-term aim is to sell on the properties after the lease with the University expires, thus providing the RCA with funds to ensure its future survival.

The design and construction therefore had to be robust and have sustainability and quality at its core. A clear separation between the Archers Hall grounds and the student housing was established, thus improving the RCA's security while avoiding overdeveloping the site. The new development was anchored to the site by incorporating large sections of the existing boundary walls into the new buildings.

The new archery range abuts a flat roofed single storey building clad in untreated European Oak boards on its garden side, which provides a flexible space for events by the RCA. Separated from Archers Hall through a glazed link, the Entrance Pavilion provides a fully accessible access from Buccleuch Street to both Archers Hall and the garden.

The massing for the student accommodation was driven by the desire to maintain the view from Archers Hall across to the Meadows park and to create a new courtyard between the residential blocks. The housing units were built using generously sized timber frames to allow the internal layout to be adjusted in the future.

The wood fibre insulation installed far exceeded the regulatory requirements of the time, while the detailing minimised air leakage through the building fabric. The specification of internal and external materials was made with durability, robustness and indoor air quality in mind.

The site-wide Sustainable Urban Drainage System was based on an attenuation layer built underneath the courtyard's permeable paving; this collects and slows down rainwater before discharging it into the drains. Building the courtyard completely flat greatly improved the accessibility across the development.

The residential heating and power needs are met by the University's Combined Heat and Power plant located in George Square and each flat is fitted with an energy display that helps the University and its students monitor energy consumption.

COMMONWEALTH GAMES ATHLETES VILLAGE
DALMARNOCK, GLASGOW

GLASGOW CITY COUNCIL

Developed by Glasgow City Council in conjunction with private sector consortium City Legacy, the Athletes' Village is a major catalyst in the redevelopment and renaissance of Glasgow's East End.

The Village has been designed to help Glasgow achieve its vision of becoming one of the most sustainable cities in Europe, in terms of reducing carbon emissions. The first phase of the project, which comprises 700 new homes (built in 700 days) and a 120-bedroom care home, achieved a BREEAM EcoHomes 'Excellent' standard.

Three hundred of the homes are for owner occupation, with 400 for rent through local housing associations. Much of the housing was occupied by first time buyers and was designed to incorporate the 'lifetime homes' concept. In this case, by allowing families to convert loft space into bedrooms as they grow. A Sustainable Urban Drainage System manages the surface water drainage, and open spaces provide a low density feel to an urban development.

The scheme incorporates an on-site Combined Heat and Power plant and it is one of the largest district heating networks installed in a residential development in the UK. In addition, photovoltaic panels and other sustainable design elements have resulted in both reduced energy bills for residents and reduced carbon emissions.

The Village has not been developed in isolation. It benefits from new and improved transport links, such as the Clyde Gateway dual carriageway, Dalmarnock train station, and several new cycle routes and lanes; state-of-the-art sports facilities are on the doorstep, including the Emirates Arena, Sir Chris Hoy Velodrome and Dalmarnock Hub community centre. A new footbridge over the River Clyde links the Village to the Cuningar Loop Riverside Woodland Park.

MACRAE HOUSING
PLEASANCE, EDINBURGH

EBENEZER MACRAE (CITY ARCHITECT 1925–46)

This block, one of few large scale inner-city schemes by Ebenezer MacRae, shows his awareness of contemporary developments in housing design in Europe whilst still keeping to the 'Traditionalist' style based firmly on the model of the Scottish tenement. MacRae was a frequent traveller on the continent, and took a leading role in the 1935 official study tour of Continental housing organised by the Department of Health for Scotland. The tour included Vienna, Paris, Prague, Berlin and Rotterdam, and the subsequent report was extensively illustrated by MacRae's own annotated sketch plans and diagrams.

MacRae's knowledge of European housing is reflected in the way the 3 and 4 storey stone fronted flats are ranged around the periphery of the 3 acre site, enclosing communal drying greens and a playground for the adjacent nursery school, built as part of the development. Perhaps the large arched pend leading to the footpath connecting Richmond Place to the Pleasance has faint echoes of Karl Marx-Hof in Vienna.

The City Architect's Department's experience in building housing within tight governmental cost limits is demonstrated in this project.

The 15 tenement stairs contain 113 flats and 5 shops, the latter facing the Pleasance and West Richmond Street. The flats contain good sized rooms with either 2 or 3 bedrooms, the standard mid-terrace plan only being varied at the corners or above the pends. The blocks vary in height from 3 to 4 storeys and further variation comes from the slope up Richmond Place and the variety of wall-head treatments; projecting eaves, dormers, parapets etc. The tenements are solidly built with reused stone street facades, chimneys and gables, and harled cavity brick to the rear.

After 80 years these houses are still very popular and well maintained, far more so than many later public housing schemes. The 'right to buy' legislation has meant that many are now privately owned. Their high density terrace form reduces heat losses and had they still been under one ownership, it would be easy to upgrade them with better insulation in lofts and walls.

Their simple familiar Scottish tenemental form and their solid robust construction have ensured their social sustainability and should see them continue as useful housing stock for the foreseeable future.

Hopetoun Terrace, Gullane.

INTER WAR PUBLIC HOUSING
SCOTLAND

VARIOUS ARCHITECTS

Although no full scale garden cities were built in Scotland between 1900 and 1939, the promotion of garden city ideas generated a lively debate in Scotland about the relative advantages of cottages over tenements for working class families. Garden city type developments increased during WW1 as efforts were made to provide suitable accommodation for incoming defence workers.

After the war, more concerted efforts were made to deliver garden city style cottages under the provisions of the Housing and Town Planning (Scotland) Act of 1919. In difficult economic circumstances, Scottish local authorities managed to build 25,000 houses throughout the country and voluntary bodies, such as the Scottish Veterans Garden City Association (SVGCA), produced another 500.

Although these outputs were disappointing in quantitative terms, the general standard of accommodation was highly impressive in quality.

Virtually all of the 1919 Act housing has survived and has been popular and well cared for over the years. The best developments have set a standard for publicly funded working class housing rarely achieved since.

Many developments, such as Mosspark and Riddrie in Glasgow and Chesser in Edinburgh, were built in the major cities, but there were smaller scale schemes of equally high quality throughout the country, such examples as Hoptoun Terrace, Gullane, designed by Dick Peddie and Walter Todd, and Seafield Crescent, Dunbar by John W. Grant.

The Dumbarton County Architect, Joseph Weekes, produced many excellent schemes, such as a group in Old Kilpatrick. Voluntary Associations were also active, the SVGCA development at Earl Haig Gardens, Edinburgh was designed by Henry and Mclennan.

Seafield Crescent, Dunbar.

EDINBURGH COLONIES
STOCKBRIDGE, GORGIE, NORTH LEITH, LEITH LINKS

VARIOUS ARCHITECTS

'The Colonies' are a model of medium density workers' housing unique to Edinburgh, built in different locations for and by the city's skilled workers. These simple stone terraces started out as charitable housing developed in the early 19th century in Pilrig and Rosebank, but the most attractive version was developed successfully through the second half of the 19th century by the Edinburgh Cooperative Building Company. A mutual development company was formed by skilled artisans, to make their own homes using their own labour, knowledge and funding, partly in response to being excluded from sites during a labour dispute. Working people directly developing houses, by pooling their resources of skills and money, was (and remains) really radical, taking ownership of their own homes when rent was the only usual option and there were no mortgages. The ECBC built over 2,000 homes and remained as a cooperative until 1945.

Their design, of rows of houses with a 'Lower' accessed from one side, and an 'Upper' accessed from stairs on the other, has proved to be an enduring way to house people in the city in attractive, green and pedestrian friendly streets, each with small gardens. The layout allows in lots of sunlight, and was a real departure from looming Edinburgh tenements, which are still the dominant built form. The distinctive external fore-stairs to upper flats were originally included to save costs but they really add to the streetscape, as attractive places to sit in the sun, while spatially separating gardens. Internally, the rooms are compact but are of a generous height with tall windows and are well laid out and proportioned.

The colonies have proven to be a hugely successful typology with none ever having been demolished and they are still in high demand throughout the city. Over time they have changed from being compact family homes to flats for young professionals, artists, or a mix of all three. Having proven to be well built and adaptable, they are not only practical and hard wearing, but have created closely knit communities with the narrow overlooked streets used for street parties in each area.

In the last years, several developers and housing associations have returned to this typology, sometimes replacing demolished 60s slab blocks that failed socially, and they have proved to be as popular as the original buildings. A great piece of simple design and construction, with the users' needs inbuilt from the start.

FAIRFIELD HOUSING
PERTH

GAIA ARCHITECTS

In 1984 Gaia were asked by the Scottish Development Agency to investigate the development of an industrial area of Perth. It rapidly became clear that the major barrier to development was the proximity to Hunter Crescent, one of the most derelict, criminalised housing estates in Scotland. It became evident that the adjacent, notorious estate was seen as a major disincentive to future industrial and commercial development. The SDA sanctioned community consultation. The brief was to work with the resident community to produce a plan for economic and physical regeneration.

Starting modestly from a few community workshops the momentum of the project built up over 2 years and partnerships were established to seek to regenerate the area. The first steps were nothing about buildings, but about rebuilding trust and self-belief in the community. It was important to

address social and economic issues as a prerequisite to improving the dilapidated and ugly physical conditions and restore self-belief and, eventually, real pride, in their place.

Gaia developed consultation tools for use by this community and others to identify, fund and action local priorities. The overriding objective was to achieve a self directed community and buildings that combine a healthy indoor climate and energy conservation.

The landscaping strategy has been an important consideration and has matured into a highly attractive scheme.

Eventually a Trust was formed and masterplanning and community development initiatives formed the basis of a phased development of mixed tenure, across a varied range of house types, spanning refurbishment and new build.

The team worked closely with residents and delivery agencies to produce integrated development proposals. Gaia designed the development vehicle – a housing cooperative – to take the project forward, training the cooperative client group which involved taking them to demonstration projects across the UK.

Gaia also put together an Urban Design Masterplan to guide physical development incorporating crime prevention and community building.

Gaia Architects went on to undertake refurbishment and newbuild at Fairfield with health and energy efficiency as key components and gained a number of design and regeneration awards.

Over 20 years the housing and industrial estates have flourished. Fairfield is now a thriving model community comprising refurbished apartment blocks and pioneering housing designed especially for allergy sufferers, indoor health and low energy use. The community is visited by many as a model for a sustainable development strategy.

Early refurbishment phases avoided toxic timber treatment. With each phase the specification became more resource efficient and environmentally benign. The area has moved from being 'hard to let' to one in very high demand. The estate won a World Habitat Commendation in 2003.

The project continually evolved and innovated becoming increasingly environmentally sound within the strictly controlled cost yardstick.

Opposite (left): Fairfield Housing Estate After
Above: Fairfield Housing Estate Before

McKenzie Court, Fairfield, Perth, 1991–93

Following on from the first two successful refurbishment phases – which housed most of those residents who remained in the area – this phase was for a combination of some identified and some, as yet, unidentified future residents. For those who were known, a series of options in layout and specification were offered, across a range of house type beyond the limitations of the 1930s layouts. For the others, the committee and the design team created as wide a range as possible and, by giving all ground floor accommodation its own front and back doors, reduced the number of flats per access stair.

A major innovation on this phase was the development of a toxin free timber specification, which was arranged to give the project a 30-year guarantee through maintaining natural ventilation to the structural timbers, rather than using CCA treatment. The existing timber was in any case of a higher quality than would have been available new.

Then moisture transfusive walls were introduced with use of high levels of cellulose fibre insulation, timber flooring rather than chipboard, organic paints and finishes and an encouragement for tenants not to use carpet or vinyl finishes.

Leslie Court, Fairfield, Perth, 1995

The design for 18 new flats took a 'passive' and bio-climatic approach to saving energy. Using a sun scoop form that also provides shelter from the wind. The flats have a low floor to wall ratio, high levels of insulation and large South facing windows to exploit solar gain and small North facing windows to reduce heat loss.

Ecological considerations were applied in the selection of materials. These included the selection of timber, impregnated with borax rather than CCA, organic and low solvent paints, and screw rather than nail fixings to allow timber floors to remain intact when uplifted or reused. Use of moisture transfusive walls with cellulose insulation on the inner skin of the timber-frame construction provided moisture control without the use of a vapour barrier and promote a healthy indoor climate.

The principles of a healthy indoor climate applied at Leslie Court were developed further at Toll House Gardens.

Tollhouse Gardens, Fairfield, Perth, 2004

The development comprises fourteen 1 and 2 bed units arranged around a car free courtyard. Parking is restricted to the entrance of the development with access via footpaths from the communal courtyard. The building fabric is moisture transfusive and materials with hygroscopic properties were used to aid moisture management and maintain relative humidity levels to restrict mould and mite survival rates. Benign materials were specified and known allergens or triggers (e.g. Formaldehyde) were avoided. Three different ventilation strategies (mechanical, dynamic and natural) were installed to allow for evaluation of their effectiveness at allergen reduction over a 2 year period.

An economic analysis looked at the implications for widespread implementation of healthy housing on savings in treatment costs and drugs. It concluded that the project fully integrated and demonstrated the inter-related benefits of the three aspects of sustainability policy – social, environmental and economic. Gaia were involved in pre-construction and post-occupancy research into Low Allergy Housing and tested allergen and relative humidity levels at the properties. This research was a precursor to the SEDA Guide 'Design and Detailing for Toxic Chemical Reduction in Buildings' authored by Howard Liddell, John Gilbert and Sandy Halliday.

The attention span of the media and politicians is short, but many of the deep transformations needed to achieve a sustainable built environment require long-term processes that offer an affordable, humane, route to a sustainable future to be recognised. Engaging stakeholders and the public is a prerequisite for this.

9–11 GILMOURS CLOSE
GRASSMARKET, EDINBURGH

ASSIST DESIGN

This multiple award winning project addresses the refurbishment of a row of listed tenement buildings to minimise CO_2 emissions and address the need for social housing within Edinburgh's World Heritage Site.

To minimise non renewable energy consumption and reduce the building's carbon footprint, the refurbishment included:

• A positive input heat recovery system.
• Environmental Modelling for maximum solar gain but minimum overheating.
• Improved U-Values minimising heat loss.
• Passive solar gain sunspaces.
• Secondary glazing to the existing sash and case windows
• Enhanced insulation was installed inside the existing stone fabric.
• A positive input ventilation system with heat recovery system.
• Extensive stone conservation to the front elevation.

A Ground Source Heat Pump supplying a communal heating/hot water system utilises site conditions whilst adhering to conservation constraints. The initial capital cost of the GSHP was higher than conventional gas central heating, but this initial cost was offset by a grant and delivers lower running and maintenance/ servicing costs.

The inclusion of sunspaces allows the opportunity to pre-warm air, resulting in reduced fuel bills. They also provide amenity and drying space in a high-density urban location. The removal of clothes drying from the core living space also resulted in reduced internal moisture, a potential contributor to poor indoor air quality, ensuring a healthier environment for the residents.

A client-commissioned thermal imaging study by the Edinburgh World Heritage Trust clearly showed massive reductions in heat loss compared to adjacent tenement properties.

The Mackintosh School of Architecture has undertaken a Post Occupancy Evaluation (PoE) research study comparing the theoretical performance of the suite of sustainable installations against their actual performance and user experiences. This study confirmed that the design measures have reduced tenants' bills enormously and helped in the optimisation of the heating and ventilation strategies to reduce fuel bills even further.

JAMES NISBET STREET
ROYSTONHILL

ASSIST DESIGN

In 1989, James Nisbet Street Cooperative inherited 200 tenement dwellings built by Glasgow City Council in the 1960s. The housing is part of a large estate to the North of the city centre on a relatively exposed South facing hillside. Amenities within the local area are basic, but there are some public transport links. Car parking is well below planning guidelines. A decision was taken to rehabilitate all the stock, exploiting passive solar gain where possible and adapting layouts to form a more suitable housing mix.

In Phases 2 and 3, 1,200mm deep South and West facing balconies were glazed in to make very cost effective sunspaces. Thermal mass is provided by the existing balcony structure. They are vented into the living space, and pre-warmed air is drawn through the dwelling by means of humidistat fans in the North facing service spaces. In Phases 1 and 2 oversized North facing windows were reduced to save heat loss. Condensing boilers were used in Phases 2 and 3 and overcladding insulation prevents cold bridging.

A major aspect of the rehabilitation work was the close relationship formed by the housing management team and architects with the existing tenants. As a result tenants have a strong sense of 'owning' the area and the property they live in.

An initial social survey was carried out to find out tenant requirements and aspirations and a new housing mix developed to accommodate these. Every household was interviewed individually by the architects using models and plans and offered choices on the following:

• gas or electric heating
• position of radiators
• position of electric wall sockets
• layout of kitchen
• colours of kitchen units and internal finishes
• variations on sunspaces (Phase 3 only)
• variation on dining space (Phase 3 only)
• other particular requirements

A follow up tenant survey showed 98% satisfaction with the accommodation.

Indigenous trees and planting reinforced by fencing and low walls create good wind drag around the site and partially protected entrances. Private garden areas at ground level encourage tenants to maintain the landscaping.

A strong tenants' committee met fortnightly with the design team to progress design ideas. Meetings were also arranged with groups of tenants from each communal close to determine communal finishes.

NICOLSON STREET HOUSING
EDINBURGH

GAIA ARCHITECTS

This project carried out for Edinvar Housing Association involved a state-of-the-art green refurbishment of a listed tenement block in the heart of Edinburgh's city centre, into low allergy affordable flats.

Gaia were commissioned to carry out a feasibility study to explore the twin areas of refurbishment and ecological design, giving particular attention to the issues associated with traditional and listed buildings where planning constraints are onerous. Gaia was subsequently awarded a contract to renovate a listed tenement block on Nicolson Street in Edinburgh into a state-of-the-art affordable, sustainable refurbishment. The development, on a very tight site, required special attention to the construction process logistics.

Energy efficiency was a major focus of the refurbishment and was seen as an important aspect in creating an affordable living environment for low income tenants. This was achieved through high levels of insulation, good airtightness levels, by installing low energy electrical fittings and by improving daylight levels in communal areas.

Emphasis was given to creating a healthy indoor climate. The refurbishment also considered community aspects, with a communal sitting area and clothes washing facilities, and amenity (particularly relevant for a building that provides no access to external space).

Specification and details were refined, following the results of an ongoing research project into low allergen/trigger environments at Gaia's Toll House Gardens project at Fairfield, Perth. All toxic materials and potential asthma and allergy triggers were removed and replaced with natural materials. Materials with hygroscopic properties and breathing walls were specified in order to aid moisture management and combat dust mite colonisation and mould growth.

The attention to moisture management and the precautionary approach was based on Gaia's European experience and took place a number of years before academic research in the UK addressed the issues. It is only now beginning to be recognised as a priority in building design.

Nicholson Street housing reflected in the Festival Theatre, Edinburgh.

NEW LANARK
NEW LANARK

DAVID DALE & RICHARD ARKWRIGHT (ORIGINAL FOUNDERS)
ROBERT OWEN

New Lanark sits in the valley of the River Clyde. It was founded in 1786 by David Dale and Richard Arkwright who built cotton mills and housing for the mill workers, taking advantage of the water power provided by the river.

By 1798 when Robert Owen was appointed manager the village was already thriving, forming the largest collection of cotton mills in Scotland. Between 1800 and 1824 Owen expanded the work of the mills and introduced a series of radical social reforms which greatly improved living and working conditions and also the efficiency of the workforce.

New Lanark was a showpiece of the industrial revolution, and came to epitomise Owen's Utopian socialism. It became celebrated throughout Europe, with many leading statesmen and reformers visiting the mills.

The mills finally ceased production in 1968. People started to move away from the village and the buildings began to deteriorate. In 1963 the New Lanark Association had been formed as a housing association and commenced the restoration of the housing. In 1970 the mills, other industrial buildings and the houses used by Dale and Owen were sold to a scrap metal company. By the mid 70s New Lanark was very run down, the buildings dilapidated and their surroundings used as a gigantic scrap yard.

In 1974 the New Lanark Conservation Trust was founded to prevent further damage or the demolition of the village. New Lanark was declared an outstanding Conservation Area in 1976 with all the buildings Category A listed. A compulsory purchase order was used in 1983 to recover the mills and other badly neglected buildings. The Trust was set up to restore the buildings and to create an economically sustainable community. The aim is to keep the residential community, to develop the income from tourism and hospitality (through the visitor centre and the hotel) and to rent some commercial property.

One of the mills spins organic wool, which is sold online. Water power is still used in New Lanark, a water turbine now providing electricity for the tourist areas of the village, any surplus being sold back to the grid. New Lanark is not a museum – it is a living and working community.

The restoration work is now largely completed at a capital cost estimated at some £25M, substantially funded by Historic Environment Scotland and other public agencies.

SUSTAINABLE BUILDINGS ARE FOR PEOPLE

Chris Butters

SUSTAINABLE BUILDINGS
ARE FOR PEOPLE

Just as society's goal is, in the words of the Bhutanese king, gross national happiness, so the ultimate goal of buildings is wellbeing. Architects have sometimes protested that if their buildings are beautiful, people will love and take care of them, and that is 'sustainable'. That's not enough; there's no excuse today for buildings that are not both economically reasonable and ecologically sensitive as well.

Scotland's famous biologist, planner and holistic thinker Patrick Geddes, virtually invented the credo of sustainable development with his triad of Place-Work-Folk, deriving from the natural sciences and his insight into the intimate interrelationships between ecology, economy and people. What does sustainable design mean in terms of society and culture? It addresses the commonalities, and the uniqueness, of people; and their needs, and their dreams. And it must do so without – to rework the Brundtland phrase – reducing the ability of future generations to meet their needs, and to dream.

To do this, architecture must respond to the triple context of time, place and person. Place is perhaps the easiest of these; it is what all ecological architecture tries to do, by a sensitive, elegant and efficient response to local environment, energy flows and resources. Adapting to time is less easy, for time is not only about durability, or buildings which can adapt and age well, but also unknowns; about what future generations may find neither functional nor beautiful. Few of us today love the brutalist techno-optimism of postwar design, yet their makers followed, as we do, a sincere and positive intention. How well will some of these 100 Scottish buildings function, and be perceived, and loved, in 100 years' time? Only our descendants can answer that.

Yet responding to people is even more challenging. It is firstly physiological: sustainable buildings must be healthy buildings. Beyond that, they must foster psychological and spiritual wellbeing. And beyond that again, buildings must respond to culture: not only for people in different countries but within the same country: young people or old people, poets or engineers, tenants or owners, use buildings very differently. Building is also a human process, not a noun but a verb; all building is both a social, an educational and indeed a political act.

Planning, constructing and maintaining buildings either fosters confidence, identity, understanding and solidarity, or it doesn't. Participation is a key; it can't always be achieved, but where it can, it is the surest guarantor of long-term sustainability.

Community matters. No mere slogan, community is our place in life. It may be ecological, and it may be rich, and it may even be beautiful, but if it is not happy, there's nothing. This, too, is the skill of sustainable planning and building – of placemaking. And for this, participation processes are not just the key, but the very doorway.

Eco architecture is well beyond its puerile metaphorical phase of buildings shaped like snail shells. It is also now well beyond its initial focus on the material aspects of sustainability alone, such as pollution or energy, that obsession with solar panels and superfluous technical hype. Solutions always work on the drawing board; but, whatever the calculations say, buildings are about human behaviour. Social science research including post-occupancy evaluations are bringing to the fore how sustainability targets are very often not being achieved, thanks to us two-legged creatures who can trash any theoretically sustainable building from day one, because we either don't understand it or don't care. Designers cannot deliver sustainability: they can only make it possible, and more likely, by solutions that are as user friendly and simple as possible. A corollary of this is passive design with a minimum of technology – Howard Liddell's ecominimalism. As Schumacher said, it takes a good engineer to make something bigger and more complicated, but a brilliant engineer to make it smaller and simpler. Efficiency with as little fuss or bling as possible. This architecture is seldom pretentious or egoistic, but quietly sensitive to its place, its work, its folk.

For the cultural, human side is the bottom line. Buildings should never receive awards on the day they open but only after several years; to be then judged not only by the bean-counters of carbon and lifecycle costs, but equally by the experienced wellbeing of the users of those buildings. Only these together – their objective and their subjective sustainability, if you like – provide the yardstick of success. Architecture demands ecological meaning, and economic meaning, but what is it without social meaning? Sustainable building arises where the rigour of ecological science meets the art of social and aesthetic quality. Where hands, head and heart achieve a kind of dance and balance together.

What is meaningful in this new paradigm is that we leave behind our specialist corners, for sustainable design makes us whole again; we embrace all people, and all of time, and all of space. We avoid rainforest timber far away on the other side of the world, and we consider intergenerational equity, far away in time. We respect the past and we care for the future; we respect our own local places, here, and we care for the places and resources and wellbeing of less fortunate people far away. Hence our motto in GAIA is about wellbeing: to design buildings that are healthy, both for people and for the planet. The eco technology? That's the easier part. But will we, humans, sustain it?

Chris Butters

EDUCATION

There was extensive modelling of orientation & layout to optimise passive solar heating and daylighting such that the windows and roof lights were carefully sized to avoid causing overheating, glare or excessive heat loss. There are real time displays of energy consumption, temperature, humidity and CO_2 levels in classrooms and community areas.

ACHARACLE PRIMARY SCHOOL
ACHARACLE, ARGYLL

GAIA ARCHITECTS

The provision of a primary school at Acharacle in Ardnamurchan, to replace the existing extended Victorian building, was part of the Scottish Government programme of school replacement. The client's design aspirations were high from the outset. Following on from tours of Norwegian and German Schools the Highland Council commissioned a 'Brief for an exemplar sustainable school' from Gaia Group in May 2004 to inform the tender process. Post Occupancy Evaluation was a fundamental part of the brief. The resulting building is quite different from those built using a private finance initiative procurement route.

Acharacle was conceived as a different – fundamentally better – way of creating places for children and adults to learn, not just a glorified shed with 'smart boards' but a place that the staff, children and community, were instrumental in designing, through a high degree of consultation. This included the colour strategy for the internal finishes and the landscape strategy. The result is a school and meeting place designed on the philosophy of ecominimalism; where solar gain and the body heat from pupils and staff is the dominant heating system. Acharacle is built from completely non toxic, renewable natural materials that do not adversely affect health. Daylighting levels are good, contributing to improving both teaching and learning. Acharacle is a place for the whole community to use throughout the year, not just for learning, but for community sports and an annual Gaelic music festival.

Acharacle was the first building in the UK to be built from Brettstapel – a glueless form of solid ('massive'), off-site timber construction that uses hardwood dowels to fix softwood posts together to create large, structural panels for floors, walls and roofs. Acharacle has a thermal performance and an airtightness performance $(0.27m^3/hr/m^2$ @50Pa) well in advance of mandatory standards. This fabric performance is in line with Passivhaus standards. Acharacle's natural ventilation strategy, which uses a combination of manually opened low level windows and sensor controlled high level windows responding to temperature and carbon dioxide levels. Avoids the need for a Mechanical Ventilation and Heat Recovery system increasingly associated with Passivhaus.

Close attention was given to moisture control through the use of moisture transfusive construction and hygroscopic finishes, including clay plaster and the exposed end grain of timber. Indoor Air Quality was a consideration in the specification, including exclusion of glue, PVC and toxic materials. New furniture was developed which minimises off-gassing to protect the very sensitive physiology of the children. No one should have to use a building that might make them ill. Efficient electrical and water conserving fittings and appliances, along with rainwater harvesting for use in toilets, further minimise resource use. CO_2 sequestration was a further consideration with over 1m kg of CO_2 sequestered in the superstructure of the building. Less than 50,000kg of CO_2 were emitted in the transport of the prefabricated, preinsulated panels to site from Austria.

NOTRE DAME PRIMARY SCHOOL
DOWANHILL, GLASGOW

PROJECT MANAGEMENT & DESIGN, DEVELOPMENT & REGENERATION SERVICES, GLASGOW CITY COUNCIL, ASSISTED BY HOSKINS ARCHITECTS.

Notre Dame Primary School, located within a residential conservation area on the edge of Glasgow University's campus, opened in 2013 following the careful refurbishment and extension of a Category C listed landmark 'parish school' building. It is home to 440 pupils and 60 nursery age children. The library, classrooms, gym, assembly hall and playground are also used in the evenings, weekends and summer holidays for education, leisure and community activities.

The 1894 school served its local community well for over a century, however, by 2010 its fabric and internal spaces were considered incompatible with modern educational requirements. It was scheduled for demolition and replacement, until the council's in-house design team successfully demonstrated that historic architecture and modern educational, social and environmental standards are entirely compatible.

Design challenges presented by the original building included a ground floor with no internal connections with the upper floor levels – it originally contained only plant, heating ductwork, storage and a janitor's flat; 4 storeys with no lift; leaky roofs and sash windows; no insulation; and an inefficient heating system.

These deficiencies were compensated by finely detailed sandstone elevations, an elegant central atrium, large windows, and spacious high ceilings.

The problematic elements of the original building were either carefully removed, or sensitively altered, with the best features conserved and repaired, and complemented by a striking new extension.

The completed project has more than double the previous floor area, operates for more than twice the number of hours per year (4654 v. 1962) and uses less than half the energy previously required. This is an eightfold improvement in efficiency. Notre Dame also provides many popular community benefits, contributes to a reduction in the city's annual carbon emission tax, and is a template for the country's rich heritage of Victorian school buildings.

COLMONELL PRIMARY SCHOOL
COLMONELL, SOUTH AYRSHIRE

ARPL ARCHITECTS

The new Colmonell Primary School is a replacement for an earlier 1970s prefab structure which had reached the end of its life. This structure was an unattractive and alien building in the village conservation area. In order to maintain the vibrancy and sustainability of the village, the local council resolved to provide a new sustainable primary and nursery school.

Colmonell is designed to cater for up to 50 primary age children in two composite classes and a nursery class of 10 children. The teaching spaces are supported by a main dining and sports hall, a central open area with library and a variety of staff spaces. The main hall and a multipurpose meeting room are available for use by the local community.

The building sits on a small site on Main Street facing South East. The design addresses issues of organisation, scale, context, landscape and biodiversity in a structure which minimises energy use. The interior spaces take advantage of naturaldaylight, natural ventilation and provide a healthy environment, free from harmful chemicals.

The plan is laid out, with staff and support areas forming a street frontage. The teaching spaces sit behind this support area with a high shared space and hall forming the core of the building. The main classrooms open to this shared space and out to the playground.

Immediately outside each class is an enclosed seating area with a water butt providing a focal point for outside teaching. The back edge of the playground is given over to a bank of raised planters for the children to use.

The cross section of the building was generated by the desire to provide a daylit, naturally ventilated, internal environment. The main roofs are flat turfed areas rising in stepped vaults over the larger central spaces. This profile gives the opportunity for stack effect to drive the natural cross ventilation and affords views out to the sky or hills from every space.

RBGE LECTURE THEATRE
ROYAL BOTANIC GARDEN EDINBURGH

SMITH SCOTT MULLAN ASSOCIATES

The project involved the comprehensive refurbishment of the Royal Botanic Garden Edinburgh's Category B listed Victorian lecture theatre to provide a contemporary facility suitable for both the organisation's own education purposes and commercial hire. A series of earlier internal alterations had compromised the quality of the space. The seating was uncomfortable and at the end of its usable life, the building services were expensive to run and unreliable, and a significant improvement in audio visual equipment was required.

The first key intervention was to remove a 1960s suspended acoustic ceiling, restoring the original full height space and exposing the existing metal roof structure and high level glazed lantern. A new timber battened ceiling introduces warmth and beauty to the room and carefully controls its acoustic characteristics. The increased ceiling height created space for new high efficiency light fittings and cutting edge audio visual equipment.

The second key intervention was to create a fully naturally ventilated space, rather than replace the existing mechanical ventilation system. Existing windows that had previously been sealed shut were fully reconditioned to provide cooling and fresh air and new, openable, timber windows linked to an automated control system were fitted to the high-level lantern.

The decision to omit mechanical ventilation and utilise a fully naturally ventilated approach has significantly reduced CO_2 emissions and future running costs. The ventilation strategy has proved to be very successful, even in summer days when the lecture theatre is fully occupied. The original radiators have been retained served by a new centralised boiler, with insulated pipework and thermostatic control valves improving efficiency.

Where possible, the existing fabric of the building was retained and upgraded rather than replaced. High quality new leadwork and slating repairs were carried out, windows have been upgraded and the opportunity taken to introduce additional insulation to reduce heat loss. This approach of re-use was continued through to the internal fittings where the hardwood writing desks from the old lecture seats were retained and used creatively to construct a new bespoke lectern.

Creative refurbishment of this building celebrates its unique garden setting, It has significantly improved its environmental performance, while avoiding the black box feel of many lecture facilities.

EDINBURGH CENTRE FOR CARBON INNOVATION (ECCI)
OLD HIGH SCHOOL, 12 INFIRMARY STREET, EDINBURGH

MALCOLM FRASER ARCHITECTS

The Centre is a redevelopment of the 18th century Royal High School in Edinburgh's Old Town with new atria, and social and teaching space, stitched between and around the historic buildings. The integrity of the historic buildings is restored but the whole delivers all the breakout and flexible working space that exemplar modern teaching and business practice demands.

The ECCI is a partnership between the three Edinburgh universities: a flagship teaching and business innovation hub for the knowledge, enterprise and skills required to create a low carbon economy. As such the building's own performance is significant and it is the first fully-listed building anywhere to receive a BREEAM Outstanding rating. Compared to other BREEAM Outstanding 'green spaceships in business parks', this represents a radical alternative and promotes the view that the achievement of a low carbon economy should start with the joyful renewal of sturdy historic buildings, rather than their replacement.

This recognition, of the importance of the integrity of the existing built environment, extends out from the building into the surrounding urban fabric. The historic Surgeon's Square (where Burke and Hare once delivered cadavers to Dr Knox's Dissection Theatre) to the rear of the Centre, is recovered and transformed from a forgotten car park to a valuable urban focus. Routes are opened up through it connecting the Centre to the Parliament, and to the general institutions and amenities of Edinburgh, by foot, providing connectivity to reinforce its sustainability.

Alongside good conservation practice the new additions are constructed from structural timber and breathing insulation, with natural ventilation assisted by the stack effect in the atrium and the University's district heating system utilised.

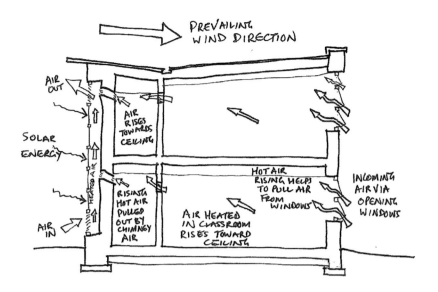

LOW CARBON TECHNOLOGY BUILDING
SOUTH LANARKSHIRE COLLEGE

AUSTIN-SMITH: LORD

South Lanarkshire College's brief was simple – design a new eight classroom teaching building that achieved a BREEAM Outstanding rating. Construction is one of the three main departments within the College and the client team wanted to experience all parts of the design and construction of a low energy building and used the process as part of their teaching curriculum.

The College initially developed a BREEAM pre-assessment for the project and included this as part of the project brief. Austin-Smith: Lord, working with Will Rudd Davidson and Cundall, developed a design which met these requirements and made best use of the natural resources on the site.

A fabric first approach to low energy design was adopted. The ground floor, external walls and roofs are all highly insulated and windows are triple glazed. The thermal mass of concrete floors, blockwork walls in the main corridor and timber insulation in the roof, provides thermal buffering during the summer months.

A natural ventilation strategy throughout the building includes thermal chimneys as key components on the South elevation. In the warmer summer months, the air passing through these chimneys rises more quickly. This air movement is used to pull warm air from the main corridor via high level ventilators. High level ventilators between the classrooms and the main corridor allow warm air to be pulled towards the corridor. The air moves more rapidly through the building as external temperatures increase.

All mechanical and electrical services use low energy fittings. The heating is provided by a ground source heat pump, linked via underfloor heating.

A 120 PkW array of photovoltaic panels on the main roof fully balances out the building's electrical demand. Low water use fittings and a rainwater harvesting system suppling water for flushing toilets, together with a Sustainable Urban Drainage System, secured all the available BREEAM credits for water use, including the innovation credit.

COMMUNITY

PORTSOY BOATBUILDING CENTRE
PORTSOY, ABERDEENSHIRE

BROWN + BROWN ARCHITECTS

Portsoy Boatbuilding Centre is a community building for the Scottish Traditional Boat Festival (STBF), located in Portsoy on the North coast of Aberdeenshire. The building replaced two derelict stores, and was partially funded by Aberdeenshire Council, Historic Environment Scotland, and the Aberdeen European Fisheries Fund.

The STBF works with local children and the wider community and stages an annual boat festival in Portsoy which draws thousands of people from around the world. Part of an ambitious regeneration programme along the waterfront, the Boatbuilding Centre follows the renovation of several other historic buildings.

A modern timber building has been slipped inside a reconstructed stone skin. Due to the historic setting no new openings were permitted in the stone walls and as a result most of the natural light comes through a ridge light which runs the length of the building.

The building is heavily insulated, and has no central heating system. All heat comes from the workshop stove, which burns waste timber from the boatbuilding activities.

A large proportion of the construction work was undertaken on site by local volunteers, which, when considering the town's distance from any population centre, resulted in a lower carbon footprint than would have been achieved through the conventional client / contractor route.

Spaces are provided in the Boatbuilding Centre for the construction of traditional boats, and the teaching of these skills.

THE BOILER HOUSE
THE HIDDEN GARDENS, GLASGOW

COLLECTIVE ARCHITECTURE

This small community building in the Hidden Gardens, at Tramway in the Pollokshields area of Glasgow, has been constructed within the existing walls of an old boilerhouse building that used to stand on the site.

The building creates a focus for a variety of garden based activities organised throughout the year, and is designed for both visiting classes of school children and local community groups. It provides a distinct, private space from the main Hidden Gardens for these activities to take place. In addition to an internal workspace there are associated kitchen, toilet and office facilities. An enclosed external garden area allows classes to take place in the open air.

Recycled materials were specified where possible. The main floor to the workspace was created from a reclaimed gym floor, including original line markings, while raised planting beds were constructed from gabion baskets filled with reclaimed bricks.

The old boilerhouse walls form most of the external walls to the new building, with the additional new walls clad in profiled aluminium reflecting the industrial history of the site.

A septic tank was also installed, to minimise the loss of original cobbles which surround both the building and gardens.

THE BIG SHED
TOMBRECK, ABERFELDY

ECOLOGICAL ARCHITECTURE LLP

The Big Shed is a community building serving a scattered rural population around Loch Tay in Highland Perthshire. The design brief was for a series of flexible spaces to be used by individuals, groups and small businesses in the community. The project demonstrates the use of locally sourced natural materials and aimed to reduce CO_2 emissions, both during construction and in use, as well as providing training in sustainable building principles for contractors and volunteers involved in the build.

The community hall is especially impressive with a double height space, visible timber trusses, timber ceiling boards, a spalted Beech timber floor and it has achieved excellent acoustics. This space is used for a variety of activities, including concerts, ceilidhs, talks, workshops, one-off celebrations and private events, such as parties, weddings and conferences, together with weekly groups and classes.

The sheltered South facing site allowed for a passive solar building, as well as offering splendid views out over Loch Tay and the surrounding mountains. The building is a simple rectangular form with a long Southfacing elevation, and ample glazing to maximise solar gain. The overhanging roof prevents internal glare from low winter sun, and shelters building users from inclement weather.

Constructed from local green Sitka and Norway Spruce, with high levels of sheep's wool insulation in the roof and walls. An internal skin of Hemcrete blocks adds thermal mass, and a wood pellet stove and solar thermal panels provide the space and water heating.

The selection of totally natural and renewable building materials, including timber, hemp, sheep's wool, rubber flooring, lime, clay, oil and lime based paints, ensured no pollution during construction, and provides an excellent internal environment.

The modest exterior does not prepare the visitor for the quality and ambiance of the interior, which has a very intimate feel, especially when the wood pellet stove is burning. The low form of the building, with its cheerful blue window frames and external Larch cladding, settles the building comfortably into its rural landscape.

GRASSMARKET COMMUNITY PROJECT
GRASSMARKET, EDINBURGH

HOSKINS ARCHITECTS

The client's brief was for a building with high quality robust finishes, minimal embodied toxins and low running costs.

Large roof lights and triple glazed windows provide natural lighting to all the habitable rooms and an extensive green roof has been installed, so that, when viewed from above, the building blends in with the adjacent kirkyard.

Internally, public areas have stone flooring, and a 300mm thick structural timber cassette system is lined in timber and reinforced boards. The structural cassettes were fully insulated to give a U-value far exceeding the Scottish Building Regulations.

Manufactured off-site within the Scottish Central Belt, from Scottish timber, reduced transportation distances and CO_2 emissions. The manufacturer's innovative robotic production line reduced waste in manufacture and the panels arrived on site complete with insulation, membranes and wiring in place, making for an efficient, clean and safe construction program on a tight urban site.

A floating ground floor provides a plenum chamber for air movement deep into the plan and this naturally ventilates the hall. Warm air is extracted at high level through vents contained within the cheeks of the roof lights.

Biomass boilers, solar-thermal panels, wind generation and photovoltaic panels were deemed unsuitable for the historically sensitive location.

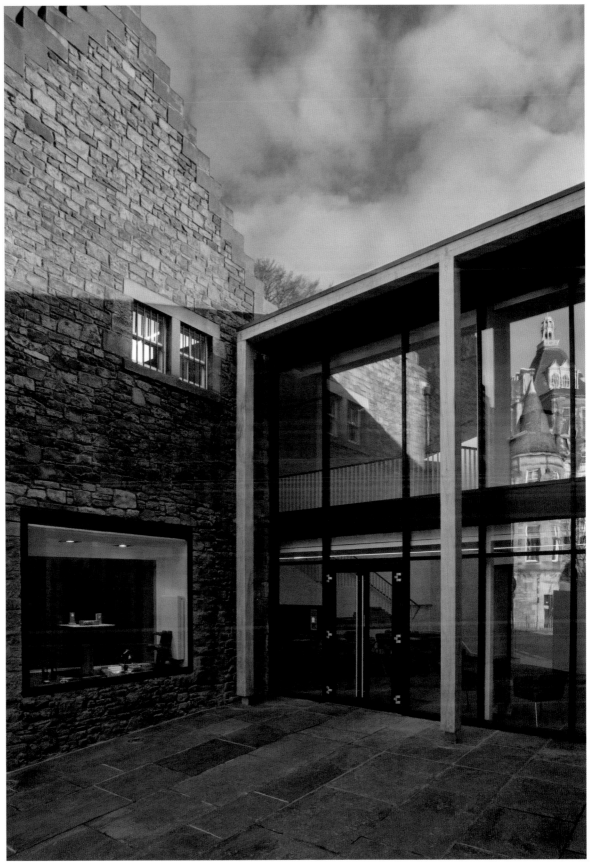

THE NOUST
ISLE OF TIREE

TOG STUDIO

'The Noust' Community Boathouse was built to preserve and reinvigorate maritime traditions of sailing, boatbuilding and boat maintenance on the Isle of Tiree.

The model by which this charitable project was delivered was highly innovative and reflected the building's purpose of sharing craft skills and knowledge. The boathouse was designed to be delivered in two phases, over two week-long 'live-build' summer schools, which would see students of architecture and engineering, and self-build enthusiasts, travel to this remote island to learn through first-hand experience how drawings become buildings.

The building was designed so that anyone could fully participate in the construction process and achieve high quality finishes. The structure consists of a series of 6m wide ply box portal frames that elevate the structural capabilities of underutilised Scottish C16 timber by attaching CNC routered plywood panels. The frames were designed to be robust, to resist fierce Atlantic gales, whilst remaining sufficiently lightweight that a small team could raise and position each frame without the need for costly lifting equipment. This structure combines the best of traditional timber-frame construction with digital fabrication technology to create an efficient structural solution that can be partially prefabricated on the mainland and assembled within a few days by an unskilled team.

Early stage collaboration between the Client, Tiree Maritime Trust, and Tog Studio made this 'unviable' project possible. Tiree Maritime Trust had a desperate need for workshop and storage facilities to save their fleet of traditional wooden boats, but had limited volunteer time and funding available to build a shelter. Through collaboration with Tog Studio, the team were able to access material sponsorship from industry, which was matched by funding from the Tiree community wind turbine and the labour of 50 visiting participants. The outcome was a bespoke community owned building, delivered for a fraction of the cost of a traditionally procured building and a new network of empowered participants who learned a lot about how buildings are made.

WIKIHOUSE
FOUNTAINBRIDGE, EDINBURGH

FOUNTAINBRIDGE CANALSIDE INITIATIVE (FCI)
JANE JONES & AKIKO KOBAYASHI

Over the course of one weekend in October 2015, more than 70 people gathered to assemble and erect a standalone community space in the heart of the 'Meanwhile' site in Fountainbridge, Edinburgh. The Fountainbridge Community WikiHouse was created by Fountainbridge Canalside Initiative (FCI) and uses an open source design that has been adapted to the particular conditions of the usage, site and budget. FCI members Jane Jones and Akiko Kobayashi led the project, which included obtaining funding, designing and testing the structure, prefabricating the components, sourcing materials (some donated), and promotion and coordination on site.

The location is a prominent brownfield plot, owned by the City of Edinburgh Council, adjacent to the canal to the West of the city centre. Last used as a brewery, the site had previously been home to the North British Rubber Company, Castle Silk Mills and various other artisan industries dating back to the early 1800s.

The WikiHouse approach represents the third industrial revolution in the rich history of manufacturing in the area.

FCI is a group of community activists and local groups who are working to ensure a viable and sustainable local community is created on the site as it is developed.

The WikiHouse is used for discussion groups, craft workshops and events and is one of a number of temporary activities prior to development starting on-site. Each activity hopes to feed into the permanent features and character of the new neighbourhood.

LITTLE BUILD
MILTON, GLASGOW

LOVEMILTON

LoveMilton is a community organisation that was first established by local residents in 2008. Gaining charitable status in 2009, LoveMilton has grown to become part of the backbone of the community, working daily to alleviate and combat social deprivation faced by many of the local residents.

LoveMilton aims to create a self-build community centre using reclaimed materials. Currently there are few local leisure facilities, minimal shops and transport links are poor. But the positive attitude and involvement of local residents has allowed LoveMilton to help the local community gain new skills, meet new people and strive to make Milton a better place to live.

The Little Build was designed as a test bed project for the larger initiatives. It was designed by 2nd year architecture students at Glasgow School of Art and constructed through several sustainable building courses, volunteer sessions and events.

The design utilises a reclaimed shipping container, recycled scaffolding planks, a sedum planted roof and homemade quark lime paint.

LoveMilton worked in partnership with SEDA to develop sustainable construction training courses through the SEDA Build School programme, including a three day green roofing course, led by green roof expert Dusty Gedge.

The sustainable building skills that volunteers gained on the Little Build will be a valuable resource for future LoveMilton community construction projects, such as the self-build training centre and the proposed Milton community centre.

DAVID DOUGLAS PAVILION
SCOTTISH PLANT COLLECTORS GARDEN, PITLOCHRY

ROBIN BAKER / GAIA ARCHITECTS

In an effort to raise awareness among the general public and promote the use of sustainable home grown timber, Scottish Enterprise and the Scottish Forest Industries Cluster Group approached Robin Baker at Gaia Architects Aberfeldy to design an innovative structure for the Scottish Plant Collectors Garden, a new garden being developed by Pitlochry Festival Theatre.

The Pavilion commemorates the significant contribution to Scottish forestry made by the 19th century explorer David Douglas, who came from nearby Scone. The Pavilion has become one of the central landscape features of the new garden, which opened to the public in 2003.

In addition to providing an exhibition space, it has hosted theatre performances and many celebrations, including weddings.

The original concept was of a 'folded leaf' used as an overarching roof form protecting the sheltered space within and below the cantilevered canopy. The combination of traditional pegged framing construction and modern sheathed framing, then informed the concept to produce the simple organic form of the building.

The timber specified was all sourced from within Scotland. The main structural posts & beams, roof decking, wall framing, cladding and viewing deck are all in untreated Douglas Fir. The roof finish is sawn Larch shingles, from untreated selected heartwood. The windows and doors have been made in laminated Scottish Oak. The floor boarding is a mixture of Ash and Elm boards.

The Pavilion has gained a great deal of interest from the press since it opened and was shortlisted in the Wood Awards 2003.

REIDVALE URBAN ALLOTMENTS & STREET-SCAPING
GLASGOW

ASSIST DESIGN

Reidvale Housing Association commissioned ASSIST to restructure the urban environment and landscaping of Reidvale Street. Following a public consultation, the project developed into two distinct phases. Firstly, the reuse of a strip of unused land and secondly, enhancing Reidvale streetscape to improve road safety. The allotments were the first new allotments postwar in Glasgow.

The first phase, completed in 2008, was the rehabilitation of land bounded by a railway to the South and overlooking tenements to the North. The client wanted to introduce a valued sustainable community resource that would visually enhance the area. Participation events had introduced the idea of creating urban allotments for local residents.

The project included repairing an existing perimeter wall, the installation of new galvanised steel fencing and the division of the site into 3 nodes. Each node has a community shed with electric power outlets and provision for further storage. The sheds are

Cedar clad externally, on a timber frame, with a natural zinc roof finish draining into water butts and a South facing veranda. There is a node for local school and nursery use and another contains raised planter beds, constructed from Baltic Pine railway sleepers in a lattice formation. Each of the 6 beds is built to varying heights to promote use by all potential users.

Phase 2 will be the culmination of the pedestrianisation of the Western end of Reidvale Street and adjoining railway bridge. The design completes direct pedestrian links with the local community centre and allotments. A number of 'moment points' are included, creating opportunities for meeting spots and pausing places that promote street activity by local residents.

By populating the streetscape, the project contributed to the creation of a stronger community, with a strong sense of identity.

TULLIS RUSSELL ENVIRONMENTAL EDUCATION (TREE) CENTRE
MARKINCH, GLENROTHES

RICHARD ATKINS

The TREE Centre hosts environmental exhibitions and activities aimed at the wider community and the brief required that it deliver the three attributes of Delight, Commodity and Firmness (cic, Vitruvius), exemplify both best practice and best process and all for a budget equivalent to, or less than, a typical community building.

The building form, thermal mass and orientation maximise solar gain, while avoiding glare and summertime overheating and this drives a passive stack ventilation system. The design's emphasis on building fabric, which has a much longer life than building services, together with a backup MVHR unit for busy periods in the winter, means a smaller, simpler wood pellet boiler is all that is required for heating. The solar thermal hot water panels which form the external balustrade, means that the boiler can be turned off in the summer and all lighting is low energy with presence detection. Water is provided by a nearby borehole and filtered in the building.

CO_2 emission reduction was a major focus for the project but this has not compromised on delivering an elegant architectural solution to a complex design challenge. Material selection makes use of low embodied energy / low toxicity / low maintenance materials, avoiding the use of applied finishes, composite materials and those with highly synthesised chemical structures which mitigates against recycling and biodegradability at the end of life. These include:

- Recycled aggregate / PFA concrete blocks
- Independently FSC certified timber
- Reused demolition materials to fill gabion baskets below straw bales
- Reused glulam beams, dance floor and mineral wool from the redundant building on the site
- Straw bale, wood fibre and recycled newspaper insulation
- Lime mortars and renders
- Natural fibre carpets
- Linoleum
- Coir matting
- Organic pigment and silicate paints
- Natural wax and turpentine finishes to timber
- Non PVCu sheathed cabling
- Bitumen / hemp roof covering
- HDPE internal waste pipes

The Scottish Government's Climate Challenge Fund contributed to the use of demolition, recycled, low carbon or sequestrating materials, which delivered a 95% reduction in embodied CO_2 emissions.

BUSINESS CENTRE FOR THE GALSON ESTATE TRUST
TOM NA BA, ISLE OF LEWIS

LOCATE ARCHITECTS

The 56,000 acre Galson Estate in the very North West of Lewis was purchased by the community in January 2007 to be managed by Urras Oighreachd Ghabhsainn (UOG) – the Galson Estate Trust. The Trust wasted no time in setting about improving conditions in the area with a range of initiatives, taking into account the unique social, cultural and environmental heritage of the area.

Locate were appointed to prepare plans for a new office building for the Trust, along with further offices to rent for local small businesses, a crofting archive / meeting area, and a local food and produce retail space. The intention was for the facilities to act as a hub for the local area. A separate standalone wind turbine contract was also initiated, which powers the building, an electric car and exports surplus power back to the grid.

The hipped roof and simple rectangular form of the building was inspired by vernacular examples where as little resistance as possible is offered to the wind. The building achieves Passivhaus levels of energy efficiency, with very good thermal insulation and airtightness, which is particularly important in such an exposed location.

With a low heat demand the building is kept warm by underfloor heating powered by a heat pump, in turn powered by the wind turbine. Mechanical Vent Heat Recovery further reduces the heat load whilst bringing in constant, warmed, filtered and controlled fresh air.

The building has been designed to be flexible in use, allowing for a number of possible occupation patterns and minimal disruption when changes are needed. Breathing walls mean that the durability of the timber is assured, without the need for chemical treatment and with almost all materials and components being easily reused, recycled or compostable, the building represents a nearly zero waste project.

As well as ensuring good energy performance, care has been taken to consider issues of health in the building with low level radiant heating, no draughts and attention to natural finishes throughout.

LAND SEA AND ISLANDS CENTRE REFURBISHMENT
ARISAIG

SAM FOSTER ARCHITECTS

This project is an example of how the sensitive refurbishment of a community building can provide an energy efficient, engaging community hub in rural Scotland. The Land Sea and Islands Centre, owned and operated by the Arisaig Community Trust (ACT) since 2012, originated as a Blacksmiths, with three small extensions added in 1999. As well as providing a community facility and historical resource for the local area, ACT support and promote sustainable development. The exhibits and the beautiful views from the Centre windows were not enough to detract from the thermal discomfort experienced by its users, with excessive draughts and the inability to heat the building above 16°C. The expense associated with the electric heating meant the building was closed throughout the winter losing a valuable community resource.

In 2014 Sam Foster Architects were appointed to undertake design work for internal upgrades to improve the energy performance. This refurbishment was promoted locally as an exemplar to showcase the use of natural building materials to improve the energy efficiency of traditional buildings.

The Mackintosh Environmental Architecture Research Unit (MEARU) undertook Building Performance Evaluation (BPE) to inform the design strategy. This included monitoring the indoor environment, electrical energy and space heating consumption. An airtightness test, thermal imaging survey and U-value measurements were all completed.

The BPE results signposted where improvements should be focused. Vapour open thermal insulation, new triple glazed easily openable windows, natural flooring and paint finishes were specified and detailed to improve airtightness, reduce heat loss and help ensure good indoor air quality. While the refurbishment was carried out the local community were frequently invited in to understand how the materials were being applied. A post-refurbishment BPE, undertaken by MEARU in December 2015, revealed impressive improvements had been achieved. Air infiltration had been reduced by 85%, thermal bridging had been virtually eradicated and U-value measurements revealed improvements of 16–63%. There was a 58% reduction in total electrical energy consumption. This meant that for the first time during the ownership of the ACT, the LSIC opened its doors during winter.

This project has further benefited the local community due to their engagement through the refurbishment process and the extended opening of a community hub that provides a warm, welcoming place to meet, share stories and absorb the fantastic coastal views.

WOODSCHOOL COMPOST TOILET
SGOIL NA CHOILE WOODS, ARDNAMUCHAN

LOCATE ARCHITECTS

Following an approach from the Sunart Oakwoods Initiative, Locate were appointed to design this standalone facility by the existing Woodschool building at Sgoil na Coille woodland in Ardnamurchan. The toilet was needed to support the main school building for day-long events. Without proper facilities, activities were restricted to half-days at the most. Forest Schools and wider outdoor learning were in their infancy at the time, but the development capitalised on the local community's capacity to host such events.

Despite being in the middle of a woodland, the tiny building and its facilities are entirely accessible and feature a sheltered area for prams, queuing and retreat from the rain. The building and the adjacent Woodschool are wholly off-grid. Hand cleansing is achieved by use of an antibacterial gel rather than water, and photovoltaic panels provide enough power for a fan to always draw air from the room into the toilet, avoiding any smells.

Composting toilets avoid a large number of environmental problems associated with conventional (water flushed) systems, not least the impact of building infrastructure in remote locations, as well as the energy and chemicals needed to treat sewage.

In addition, as long as poo and pee can be separated – as they are here – the poo makes for excellent compost once rotted down with the sawdust mulch, while the pee is mixed with captured rainwater (a ratio of approximately 1:20) to make what is an excellent fertiliser. Apart from the actual compost toilet, everything else in the building was made from wood sourced immediately around the site by the local contractors, who set up a mobile sawmill on site. Everything that could be made of wood was designed to maximise what could be sourced locally – the structure, internal and external linings are timber, including a horizontal larch plank roof. No chemical treatment was applied to any of the timber.

Given the generally conservative nature of the British to all things toilet based, it was agreed that the inside of the room must be as attractive as possible, to help offset any natural reluctance. In addition to being finished beautifully inside, an eye level window ensures this is a rural loo with a view.

GAIRLOCH AND LOCH EWE ACTION FORUM (GALE) VISITOR CENTRE
GAIRLOCH

MAKAR

This visitor/community centre for GALE is located on a coastal site in the heart of Gairloch. The building was designed to meet GALE's requirement for a multifunctional building that would set an environmental benchmark for new buildings in the Gairloch area. It was a brownfield site, the former site of the Gairloch Sands Hotel.

The building, which extends to 240m², contains a small café, retail area and exhibition space, along with an office for GALE and classroom areas that are leased to the University of the Highlands and Islands for teaching purposes.

The building was the first commercial building designed to Passivhaus certification standard in Scotland. The heating is provided by means of passive solar and internal heat gains from equipment and users, in conjunction with a mechanical ventilation and heat recovery system. A woodburning stove provides backup in times of extreme weather conditions. Water is heated by solar thermal panels, with an electrical immersion heater boost system. Drainage, water and electricity services are all provided by mains utilities. The construction is predominantly Scottish grown untreated timber.

The building has a Douglas Fir post and beam structure and Sitka Spruce wall panels, with cellulose insulation and durable external European Larch cladding. All windows are triple glazed and accredited for use in Passivhaus buildings. Airtightness is key to meeting the Passivhaus standard and all joints in the internal Oriented Strand Board lining were taped with proprietary airtightness tapes before being finished with plasterboard. The Centre was developed as one component of a placemaking master plan for the Achtercairn area.

The Centre is a good example of a contemporary community owned and operated building, which has been designed to provide the community with flexible spaces. The Centre was well received in the community and is heavily used.

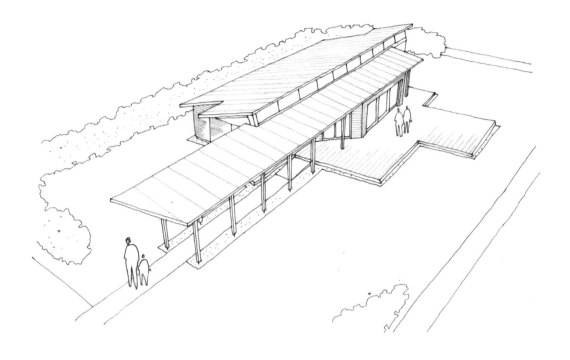

145

SOCIAL CAPITAL

Sandy Liddell Halliday

Buildings have a crucial impact on the physical and economic health and wellbeing of individuals, organisations, communities and society. For some individual buildings this influence can be for good or ill.

A sports facility designed with excellent indoor air quality is inarguably a human right – a healthy building for healthy pursuits. Provide optimised daylight and it encourages optimised use. Make it attentive to energy efficiency, and the maintenance needed to keep it running, and it will deliver operating costs at levels that make sport an affordable pastime for everyone, enhancing the health of a community. Provide it with timely, affordable, inclusive and accessible transport and, in days where we are increasingly seeing the move to fitness classes on prescription, it becomes a genuine social asset. Provide the sports facility with a manager who understands and cares about the needs, requirements and aspirations of the community, and plans to meet these, and you have a vehicle of sustainable development. Simply – making tomorrow better than today.

So, despite the title of this publication, a sustainable building cannot be considered in isolation from the people who use and manage it, nor the buildings around it. The spaces and connectivity between buildings are as important as the buildings themselves. Good design facilitates connections between people and contributes to strong neighbourhoods with a sense of community. If a place is properly designed then it will contribute to building social capital and help a community to support itself and be 'the glue' that holds individuals together as a community. Research suggests that when a community has strong social capital, wellbeing improves and deteriorating ill health lessens. This is sustainable building.

'Social capital describes the pattern and intensity of networks among people and the shared values that arise from those networks.'

Sadly, sustainable building is still marginalised in Scotland. Sustainability is perceived as a restraint on development, rather than a justified restraint on inappropriate development. Many buildings and built environments contribute to ill health and disaffection, to alienation and excessive financial liability. They are unwelcome and undesirable. They impose burdens on occupants and the environment by making people dependent on private transport. They fail to support biodiversity and protect the environment, which is short sighted and irresponsible. They are increasingly unaffordable. Where they fail to support and nourish communities, then they also embed long-term social costs. Given the problems in many communities, significant improvements are clearly possible and urgently necessary. In Scotland we have an international exemplar – Fairfield, a transformed estate and winner of a World Habitat Award – that could teach much to those intent on pulling down failing estates rather than working with them to generate social, environmental and economic capital.

The Scottish planning framework and regulatory standards impose little requirement on developers to address environmental needs and even less on social issues beyond a roundabout here or a pavement there. At best it gets a tokenistic nod, usually around energy systems, resulting in eco-bling. Or it might chase points and prizes – adding cost but not value – and reinforcing the perception of sustainability as a luxury issue rather than an opportunity for improvement for all.

No one in Scotland appears to be challenged to look at economic sustainability in the built environment that might deliver some joined-up thinking rather than absurd corporate profits. Yet as Jaime Lerner, the Mayor of Curitiba – listed as one of the most sustainable cities in the world – has said, 'If you want creativity, cut one zero from the budget. If you want sustainability, cut two zeros!'

Urban design is an area where Scotland has significant international precedent, through the reputation and writing of Ian McHarg, but approaches to placemaking and housing provision in our neighbour countries are ahead of us in many respects. They are actively seeking to design sustainable settlements and create sustainable communities by consideration of the natural environment, resource effectiveness and flexibility; space is used to generate interaction and inclusivity and accessibility to facilitate intragenerational and intergenerational equity. Those that place client involvement (including those in housing need) at the forefront of development strategies, rather than leaving decisions to a few centralised and private organisations, are proving extremely successful in building successful communities in Malmö, Culemborg, Berlin, Vauban, Freiberg and Tübingen. They know that good design facilitates good behaviours.

Sustainability in Scotland is still counter-cultural and we must continue to raise awareness of all the under-represented aspects of the sustainability agenda – toxicity, responsible science, society, equity, resources, pollution, waste, technology and an unsustainable economic system – the sustainability underdogs that still receive scant attention. There is a wealth of pioneering work – on communities, materials, timber, indoor health and a world first accreditation scheme in sustainable design – that should see Scotland leading the world.

I had humble beginnings and consider an agenda that supports affordable, healthy and resource efficient buildings with good access to a safe public realm and public transport, and enhances biodiversity, to be a fair objective. The best time to start has gone. The second best time is now.

Sandy Liddell Halliday
Gaia Research

HEALTH & WELLBEING

THE SHEILDS CENTRE
POLLOCKSHIELDS, GLASGOW

ANDERSON BELL CHRISTIE

Located in the East Pollokshields area of South Glasgow, the Shields Centre involved the construction of a new health centre to accommodate two existing local general medical practices, as well as social work and community health partnership facilities.

East Pollokshields has a rich demographic mix with more than 30 different languages spoken. A sensitive design was required to meet the needs of the entire community successfully.

Centred round a bright, airy, double-height waiting and reception area, short wings containing the consulting rooms lead off the main space. The upper floor contains a further smaller waiting space, as well as the social work and community health partnership facilities.

Externally, a community garden provides both a link between the building and the neighbouring community centre and encourages a feeling of ownership of the building by the local community. The garden showcases food growing techniques, which promote healthy living, making an important link between food and health.

Artwork has been incorporated within the building fabric in the form of a screen along the front of the building's elevation and decorative motifs are incorporated into glazed screens internally.

GIRVAN COMMUNITY HOSPITAL
GIRVAN

AUSTIN-SMITH: LORD

Girvan Community Hospital is located on a prominent site on the edge of this coastal town in South West Scotland. The Hospital is integrated with the townscape, which is predominately of traditionally single storey vernacular construction and it represents a move away from multistorey, rigidly planned hospitals.

Extensive community and stakeholder consultations were undertaken to ensure that all aspects of social and environmental sustainability were carefully considered. These included the low maintenance planting regime, protection of the nearby river embankment and the integration of local public footways, both new and existing.

From inception, one of the key elements of creating a contemporary and modern building was to minimise the carbon footprint and ongoing operational costs of the Hospital.

As a starting point, the design philosophy was to utilise as much natural ventilation and lighting as possible to enhance the patient, visitor and staff experience, supplementing this through the use of renewable technologies.

Studies were undertaken early in the process to determine the most appropriate technologies and to build in their capital cost from the outset. The increased capital outlay was justified by demonstrating that this would be more than recouped over an operational life cycle of 20 years. Conservative estimations suggest that a saving of around £1.6m will be achieved.

A 30m, 100kW, wind turbine was incorporated as an integral part of the building and has a prominent location within the landscape, acting as a focus for the Hospital's main internal and external circulation. Other features, such as, low energy lighting with daylight control, trace heating of direct hot water supply pipework (to avoid a recirculating system), motor room less lifts, infrared controlled taps and WCs, heat recovery in main plant areas and a full environmental monitoring system, which can be remotely monitored, have also been included.

CENTRE FOR INTEGRATED CARE
GLASGOW

MACMON CHARTERED ARCHITECTS

The Centre for Integrative Care focuses on complementary care and offers physiotherapy facilities. The ambition to achieve a new, purpose built Centre commenced in the late 1930s and in 1995, through a new initiative led by Dr David Reilly, Macmon Chartered Architects were appointed following an open design competition.

The central requirement of the client's brief was for the design to achieve a place of healing and beauty, commensurate with homeopathic care philosophies. Best practice strategies for energy use and sustainable design had to be identified and implemented. Cost limits were stringent and set below a normal yardstick for accommodation of this type.

The design concept was to integrate building into a landscape setting and, in so doing, harness the therapeutic benefits of natural light and visual stimulus in support of a holistic concept of care and healing. This principle is most evident in the consulting rooms where full height, glazed screens give views and direct access to decks, sitting areas and gardens.

The plan arrangement is, in essence, a courtyard form, surrounding a therapy garden space. The built form is, for reasons of cost, principally rectilinear. Strategic, curvilinear walls, finished in coloured render, have been introduced to relieve this expression and to reflect nature. The split, monopitch roof, with clerestory, provides natural light and ventilation to corridor areas. The same arrangement is also intended to exploit passive solar gains from low winter sun.

The Centre delivers a high quality, patient focused service which has been evidenced by patient and staff feedback:

'One of the reasons I wanted to work here is because of the building. It is light, airy and welcoming and the sense of space is extravagant. The best thing about working here is opening the windows and listening to the birds singing as I work.'

'Thank you so much for everything you have created at the hospital. I wonder if you realise how important it is for those of us who depend upon its environment to calm us, strengthen us, and then send us out into the world to cope for another while.'

The building's unique and high quality design has been recognised with a Dynamic Place Award.

ROYAL COMMONWEALTH POOL REFURBISHMENT
EDINBURGH

S&P ARCHITECTS

The multiple award winning Category A listed Royal Commonwealth Pool in Edinburgh is affectionately named the 'Commie Pool' and was designed by Robert Matthew Johnson Marshall Architects for the 1970 games. The original commission was for a building to accommodate a 50m swimming pool, diving pool, training pool, fitness suites and indoor rowing tanks. They were subsequently used again for the 1986 Games. In 2006 a £37m sustainable refurbishment programme commenced to bring the Commie Pool back to its former glory, to be used to host diving events during the 2014 Commonwealth Games. The refurbishment had to balance the requirements of the City of Edinburgh Council's sustainability policy with the need to maintain a public facility, while respecting the listed status of the building.

During refurbishment the building and its building services underwent major changes, including the expansion and relocation of the 50m pool, construction of a new diving pool and installation of moving floors to vary the depth of pool water.

New ventilation and heating systems were installed, along with new filtration systems to provide improved water quality. Recycled glass filter media has been used in the filter vessels, providing lower water consumption and allowing the filter media to remain in the filter for the life of the vessel, unlike traditionally used sand requiring replacement every 5 years. The preheating of the pool water is provided by a 500m^2 solar thermal array, fitted over the uppermost roof. The waste water from poolside showers is collected and cleaned in the greywater recycling plant located in the basement; this clean water is then used for flushing toilets within the building.

The refurbished building was officially reopened in 2012. The Commie Pool continues to host competitions at various levels and welcomed the Team GB swimming team, who selected the Royal Commonwealth Pool to be their training camp ahead of the 2012 London Olympics due to the exceptional water quality.

MCLAREN COMMUNITY LEISURE CENTRE
CALLANDER

GAIA ARCHITECTS

This £3.2m leisure centre was commissioned in 1996 and received research support from the DTI and Sportscotland. It was designed with a 20m pool, sauna and jacuzzi, sports hall, climbing wall, squash courts, fitness rooms, indoor bowling hall, café and associated facilities. The aim was to support Sportscotland's policy of 'healthy buildings for healthy pursuits'.

It features the use of healthy materials and an innovative ventilation technique known as dynamic insulation. This involves drawing air very slowly into the building through the cellulose insulation in the ceiling, effectively recovering heat, whilst also filtering the air. It creates a fresh and healthy indoor environment in large spaces and also saves energy. Lack of intake ductwork has health benefits and there is an associated reduction in plant cost. It is the largest building in the world to use the technique

and the first building in the world to use it for a swimming pool.

The design followed a number of years of research by Gaia into moisture and air transfusive wall and ceiling systems. Significant care was taken to achieve airtightness and also to ensure delivery of a benign materials specification to ensure a healthy indoor climate.

The building was the subject of a post completion evaluation of the performance. Gaia Research monitored the key innovative energy features of the building for two years – demonstrating how the dynamic insulation performed and was also able to undertake significant optimisation. Some of the spaces have since been reallocated and adapted to new uses as sports preferences have changed. The dynamic insulation continues to perform as intended.

GLENTRESS VISITOR CENTRE AND MASTERPLAN
TWEED VALLEY FOREST PARK

GAIA ARCHITECTS

Glentress forest lies at the heart of the Tweed Valley Forest Park, and is a centre of excellence for mountain biking. The increasing popularity of mountain biking has seen a significant rise in visitor numbers creating unwelcome pressure on the area. Gaia Architects were lead consultant for a major master planning study for the forest, and were then commissioned to design a new visitor centre and HQ.

Working in close conjunction with the Forestry Commission Scotland and other key partners, the design team analysed the existing market conditions, site infrastructure and development opportunities within the forest. The resulting report put forward visionary ideas for a mixed social/recreational/leisure/commercial development, as well as proposals aimed at increasing opportunities for access by the general public. This allowed diversification from strictly commercial forestry to a sustainable natural woodland.

Strategic guidance was also given regarding the potential use of sustainably sourced timber and resources from within the local area, together with guidance on a phased development programme which included other buildings in the forest. The proposed development of the area builds on the existing success, as well as increasing opportunities for other users.

The choice of all materials used in the scheme was driven by a desire to minimise any adverse environmental impact on the health of the end users. This has been achieved without compromising the building's performance or lifespan. Specific materials include clay plaster to regulate indoor air quality and moisture levels and linoleum to maintain a hygienic environment, while preventing off-gassing within the internal spaces, commonly associated with comparable plastic or rubber products.

Glentress was awarded a Gold star rating in the Green Tourism Business Scheme and shortlisted for both the 2011 Andrew Doolan Award and the 2012 Edinburgh Architectural Association's 'Building of the Year' Award.

ARTS & LESUIRE

Loch Leven Heritage Trail:
Viewpoint

Loch Leven Heritage Trail:
Birdhide

LOCH LEVEN HERITAGE TRAIL
LOCH LEVEN, PERTH AND KINROSS

ICOSIS ARCHITECTS

The Loch Leven Heritage Trail is a unique route linking the natural, historic and cultural heritage around the perimeter of Loch Leven. Level and barrier free, the Trail is suitable for walkers of all ages and abilities, for cyclists, for wheelchair users and motorised scooter users. Icosis Architects designed two small award winning structures for The Rural Access Committee of Kinross-shire (TRACKS) and Scottish Natural Heritage.

The first, a new bird hide on the West bank of the loch, South of Kinross, was completed in 2011 and sits on the water's edge. This required an innovative structural design and construction solution. The design is part hide, part bridge and part screening, all constructed from Scottish Douglas Fir and Larch. Viewing apertures are lined in Oak, also used to form shelves and benches.

The foundations for the hide sit on the shoreline of the Loch, which required a temporary water filled coffer dam to enable the installation of the three precast concrete bases. Two large Douglas Fir beams are bolted to these bases, onto which the bridge and hide are secured.

The hide was constructed in panels off-site, in order to reduce construction time and minimise disruption. The bridge is offset to make the entrance oblique – more of a discovery – and to line through with the island in the loch, and framing the view of Lochleven Castle when viewed from the bridge.

The second structure, a viewpoint located near the Royal Society for the Preservation of Birds reserve at Vain Farm, was installed as part of the final phase of works in 2014 to complete the 13 mile Heritage Trail.

The trail is partly cut into the hillside and earth has been banked up against a new drystone wall to provide shelter from the prevailing wind. The wall is constructed from the remains of a nearby derelict wall and built around a steel frame which supports splayed Douglas Fir roof timbers. Hit & Miss Scottish Larch boards are used in a similar way to the bird hide and provide a wind break and separation between trail and the viewing area.

Loch Leven Heritage Trail:
Viewpoint

ARBROATH ABBEY VISITOR RECEPTION BUILDING
ARBROATH

SIMPSON & BROWN

Simpson & Brown won a competition to design the Arbroath Abbey Visitor Reception Building in 1999. The scheme included a new building with visitor facilities, a retail area, audiovisual exhibition space and viewing gallery, together with external landscaping and new interpretation throughout the Abbey site.

In response to the challenging and sensitive site, the new building form is a layered 'soft' horizontal building, contrasting with the high vertical mass of the Abbey. To achieve this, the building steps back in three volumes, slowly rising up, each space within gaining height and light until it finally cantilevers over the rear graveyard wall, affording views of the Abbey behind. This view of the Abbey grounds is the key to the design and helps visitors to understand the layout of the Abbey buildings before they set out to explore them. The road leading to the Abbey was closed and the entrance area was pedestrianised.

In order to minimise environmental impact the building makes use of natural low energy and toxicity materials such as stone and timber. The timber structure is a mixture of Douglas Fir, Larch and Oak, assembled off-site. Roof trusses are simple and elegant, mixing traditional and modern materials. The timbers for the curved section of the roof were selected from those parts of individual trees which match the required profile, thus avoiding bending and the use of glued and laminated beams.

The roof is covered with sedum, a layer of vegetation sitting on a mineral wool blanket which supports the roots and stores water, enabling the rock plants to survive during dry periods. This was chosen for aesthetic and practical reasons as the most appropriate low impact, self maintaining method of covering the large low pitched roof structures. Its appearance will change with the seasons, reflecting the surrounding landscape.

ABBOTSFORD VISITOR RECEPTION BUILDING
ABBOTSFORD, MELROSE

LDN ARCHITECTS

Abbotsford, on the banks of the River Tweed, is the creation of Sir Walter Scott (1771–1832), one of Scotland's greatest writers. The new visitor reception building and car park sit in this historic setting. As designs were developed during the planning process, the proposal was presented to the local community councils, A&DS and other stakeholder groups.

The building is laid out with the reception, shop and interpretation space close to the entrance on the ground floor, and a café and terrace on the first floor overlooking Abbotsford. Circulation is kept to the car park side of the building to allow all other spaces, including the exhibition area, to be oriented towards Abbotsford.

Constructed almost entirely in timber, the two-storey building is partly built into the hillside to reduce its scale. Timber, left untreated wherever possible, is used to form every aspect of the building: structure, cladding, linings, fixtures and fittings. The extensive use of timber acknowledges it is one of the few truly sustainable construction materials.

The building's compact envelope is highly insulated and when tested for air infiltration achieved a value of 2.64 m³ / hr/m² @ 50 Pa.

The wall construction is breathable, both to control the building's internal environment and to avoid those defects associated with the long-term impact of water trapped in a building's fabric during construction.

The flat roof is finished with a sedum blanket, minimising the impact of the building, both 'recovering' the natural ground lost due to its construction and by reducing rainwater run-off by 40%. Rainwater is stored in a reclamation tank and reused to flush the WCs.

An environmental control strategy was developed to minimise the extent of installed plant and overall energy consumption. Underfloor heating is provided by a ground source heat pump connected to bores holes under the car park. All main rooms are naturally ventilated and a mechanical vent heat recovery system serving the exhibition space, recovers heat from the toilet and kitchen extracts.

Glazed walls let in as much natural light as possible to reduce the need for artificial lighting and energy saving lights controlled by motion detectors are installed throughout the building.

LOCH LOMOND PARK CENTRE
LUSS

DALLMAN JOHNSTONE

Dallman Johnstone Architects won a Loch Lomond Park Authority competition in November 1993 for the Park Centre Luss, a contemporary building capable of making a significant architectural statement, whilst respecting its lochside location and Conservation Village surroundings. Inspired by local building traditions, it contains a shop, exhibition area, audio-visual room and toilets on the ground floor. A separate entrance leads upstairs to the Park Rangers' offices.

High visitor numbers meant the building needed to be carefully designed for robustness, longevity and low maintenance. High quality natural materials were used: slate, stone and timber. While the entrance elevation appears solid, inside is a bright, double height space. Locally sourced Oak and Elm are used internally and externally.

The steel frame structure allows the external wall to be fully glazed in places. Influenced by buildings in Luss Conservation Village, a pitched roof was chosen. Slate quarrying, used in roofing, was a local industry. Reopening the quarry was investigated but not feasible. Deep roof overhangs provide shelter, both at the entrance and glazed gable facing Loch Lomond.

Traditional shapes are interpreted in a modern way. The diamond leaded windows of the older cottages inspired the small diamond windows, both internally and at the entrance. Window positions and roof overhangs were determined by the views. From a diamond window you look towards the village, whilst the audio visual projecting window provides views of Ben Lomond. For the main joinery work, Scottish Sycamore, Oak and Elm were selected. Sycamore panels at the reception desk were worked by hand, enhancing their natural shape, supported by Elm posts and hand-cut metal lacquered brackets. The main desk worktop was made from Oak. Heathers inspired the interior colours. A specifically designed carpet and individual seats created a warm and comfortable audio-visual room, which was designed to also be used by the local community.

All buildings have to respond to change. Since completion as a visitor centre, the building has undergone several changes of use, initially becoming a soap making factory and shop and recently, a restaurant. Whilst the interior has changed, the exterior design of the building has remained unchanged. This project was chosen as 1 of 4 projects to represent the best of Scottish architecture on the RIAS website homepage for 4 years in the 1990s.

GLENCOE VISITOR CENTRE
GLENCOE

GAIA ARCHITECTS

Sensitively integrated into a beautiful site in the mountains of Western Scotland, this award-winning project sums up much of what Gaia Architects has come to stand for. In the Glencoe Visitor Centre one finds a wide range of green solutions. This does not mean lots of conspicuous ecotechnology, but design based on a real understanding of site ecology, indoor climate, energy, water management and landscape. The result is quiet, unpretentious and totally fitting. There are many details that the visitor may not notice, but which contribute to a thoroughly green architecture because genuinely sustainable design is complex and subtle.

The aim was to replace the existing centre, which was poorly located in a sensitive area of the Glen and was considered to be contributing to the undermining of the natural beauty of the area. The brief was for a Visitor Management Facility with the lightest footprint it was possible to have in Glencoe – one of the most visited parts of Scotland's natural landscape – to meet the demanding requirements of the National Trust for Scotland to conserve, whilst providing access. Conceived by Howard Liddell as a clachan, a reference to the local tradition of a collection of small building volumes, the architecture expresses a quietly modern, harmonious regionalism.

Early ecological buildings were often clumsy or backward looking in style or overloaded with eco technology, which had little real effect. But gimmicks are not exciting in the long term. Architecture must be sensitive to its context, attractive, and lasting. It must also be healthy for its users. Here, the attention paid to natural materials and indoor climate is radical, but the result is a building that does not impose as being strange, technically complicated, or difficult to manage.

The Centre addresses all aspects of an ecological design brief, from careful site integration and minimal adverse landscape impact, to biological water treatment, energy conservation, passive solar design, renewable energy supplies, non-toxic material use, flexibility – and delivered at a reasonable cost.

Glencoe was a reasonably priced building to construct; and the energy and maintenance costs are half that considered to be normal. It also demonstrates 'ecominimalism', the principle that ecological buildings do not need masses of technology. The resources needed both for producing and servicing buildings can be greatly reduced by simple ecological solutions and above all, good integration. 'Walk lightly on the earth' could be a motto for the Glencoe Centre – it almost seems as if it always should have been there. Sensitive to its place and time, the ecological footprint of this building complex is very light indeed.

As part of the landscaping commission, the site of the original centre was returned to nature and now few would know that it ever existed.

TROSSACHS DISCOVERY CENTRE
ABERFOYLE

DALLMAN JOHNSTONE

The Trossachs Discovery Centre is located in the heart of Aberfoyle village. Over time the focus in the village had moved from the Main Street to the tourist car park next to the Centre. Prone to flooding and with challenging changes of level, the site was replanned to create an area for events to the South of the Centre.

The Centre replaced a previous small Tourist Information Centre and public toilets and provides additional retail and potential business space. Located on a narrow site, the design also had to incorporate a covered bus stop.

Local contractors and materials were used wherever possible. A solid Douglas Fir structural frame was chosen over steel in part as Aberfoyle lies within the Queen Elizabeth Forest Park. This choice was not without difficulties – in particular the high moisture content – but it is a long life, low maintenance non-toxic material from a local sustainable source. Timber is important to the Scottish economy and it also uses less energy during fabrication than steel and sequestrates carbon. The character of the large timber frame is enhanced by the shakes, which are an inevitable

consequence of drying out large baulks of timber, giving the building a mature appearance. Externally, timber boarding reflects that found on many of the existing buildings in the Main Street.

Aberfoyle lies on the Highland Boundary Fault and after careful research, the slate quarry above the village was reopened to provide material for the external walls. The green/grey rough textured slate contrasts with smooth red sandstone quoins. To achieve the random rubble design, old walling techniques had to be relearnt, tilting the stone outwards to shed water away. Selecting stones becomes a three-dimensional puzzle to achieve the horizontal bedding. The effort is well worth it as it contributes immensely to the townscape of Aberfoyle.

Overall the Centre achieved the client's brief of promoting the protection and preservation of the local environment.

When the building was 10 years old, UK Trade & Investment chose it as one of 6 tourism projects to showcase the Best of British Expertise. It was chosen for its sustainability.

SCOTTISH STORYTELLING CENTRE
HIGH STREET, EDINBURGH

MALCOLM FRASER ARCHITECTS

Cultural reuse and regeneration is as important a driver for sustainability in the built environment as physical. The SSC establishes a place for storytelling as a freestanding contemporary artform that is woven into the rich literary history of Edinburgh's Old Town. Its location at the Netherbow Port, incorporating the iconic, historic John Knox House and representing the Netherbow's historic bell, supports storytelling's status as 'gateway' art, while the project's urban weave of court, close and garden recovers the mediaeval townscape of Edinburgh, whose creative and social interaction sparked its writers, artists and thinkers.

The virtues of physical reuse were also paramount, the project not only repairing and renewing John Knox House and associated historic fragments, but reusing the 1970s fabric of the site's previous building, rebuilding and refitting to greatly improve fabric and energy performance, with heating and ventilation low energy, including exploiting the stack effect of the storytelling court and maximising daylight into the court. Natural materials were used throughout and acoustics tuned to the needs of the storytelling theatre and court.

The Centre's success has been to promote a new use within the Old Town, that connects back into history but is contemporary, that attracts both locals and visitors and that has evolved ground-up but been embraced by the establishment. It has brought alive both the artform and the particular urban form of the mediaeval city, weaving them together to embrace place and culture and represent them to the world.

WATERSTON HOUSE
ABERLADY

SIMPSON & BROWN

Waterston House, the headquarters for the Scottish Ornithologists' Club in Aberlady, East Lothian, was completed in June 2005 and houses the most comprehensive ornithological library in Scotland.

The building's design adopted a simple form and was designed to have a minimal impact on its surroundings. It accommodates a library, lecture hall, exhibition space, offices and archive storage.

Untreated green Douglas Fir provides the main structural frame, which uses traditional pegged and tenon jointing – the wall framing, sarking and battens are Sitka Spruce. Externally, the wall cladding is untreated Larch, and internally the flooring in the entrance and gallery space is Oak, all of which is home grown and largely provided by the Forestry Commission Scotland.

Internal and external materials are durable, robust and maintain good indoor air quality.

The surrounding landscape was specifically designed to encourage local birdlife, incorporating a pond which has varying water conditions, from fast moving to still, to provide differing habitats for birds. The pond also acts as a storage reservoir for rainwater collected from the roof, and is integrated with the services strategy for the building.

FORSINARD LOOKOUT TOWER
FORSINARD, SUTHERLAND

ICOSIS ARCHITECTS

Forsinard Lookout Tower was commissioned by The Peatlands Partnership and sits on the edge of a bog pool system forming part of the Dubh Lochan Trail in the Flows National Nature Reserve, Sutherland.

A particular feature of blanket bogs is the pool systems, which can create impressive patterned areas when seen from above. This is one of the classic views of the peatlands but one which is rarely accessible in the Flow Country. A key purpose of the tower is to enable visitors to experience this striking view.

The tower also highlights the need to conserve peatland habitats to mitigate climate change and, given its location within an area of Dark Skies, it also provides a platform for stargazing.

The exact location was carefully chosen with regard to its impact on the landscape; how it would sit within the pattern of bog pools, how it would be viewed from different angles and how the optimum

viewing height for the structure would appear in the wider landscape.

As a single organic form clad in locally-sourced timber, the design concept is simple in providing a blank elevation to the public road and opening up to provide views to the West, focusing visitors' attention across the pools and the natural landscape beyond.

In order to minimise disruption to the peat, the structure is built of slender hollow piles driven to a solid base around 4m below the surface of the bog.

High quality, robust and durable materials were used throughout: including untreated Scottish Larch supplied by the Forestry Commission and used as hit & miss battens to clad the timber and steel structure, both inside and out; locally sourced Caithness stone for the ground floor and non-slip Scottish Larch boarding for the upper viewing deck.

ALPINE HOUSE
ROYAL BOTANIC GARDEN, EDINBURGH

SMITH SCOTT MULLAN ASSOCIATES

This is the first new glasshouse to be built in the Royal Botanic Garden Edinburgh for over 30 years and the only one in Britain dedicated to growing alpine plants in a tufa rockscape.

The key design drivers were to respond to the cold, windy, yet bright, mountain environments required by these plants, while providing a distinctive structure that will act as a contemporary landmark in its own right, within the stunning garden setting.

The galvanised steel and glass structure modifies the microclimate by providing shelter from excessive rain, while transmitting maximum light and increasing wind speed at plant level. Stainless steel mesh around the South side of the structure provides protection from pests, including cats and large birds.

The visual concept evokes the nature of plants opening to the sun, while reflecting both the strength of the mountains and the sharp edges of frost shattered rock so prevalent in alpine settings. The Design Team worked closely with the Garden's horticultural staff to understand and respond to the plants' exacting requirements.

The plants are grown in a porous rock called tufa, which is formed from calcium carbonate deposited from fresh water springs. The North face of the building is a cavity wall faced with the tufa rock and filled with compost material and has an automatic watering system.

The primary structural steel elements were prefabricated and pre assembled for testing, before being galvanised and brought to site for final erection. Galvanised steel was selected as the primary material for the project to ensure longevity, enable the structure to be expressed and provide a cost effective solution.

The structure, glazing and framing is entirely recyclable, emphasising the sustainable agenda set as part of the brief. The glasshouse requires no heating, cooling or ventilation. The structural design includes a dramatic 8m cantilever formed in tapering beams, creating a canopy over the main entrance to the glasshouse.

'This small but striking project provides the Royal Horticultural Garden Edinburgh with a dramatic 21st century addition with a high environmental performance, which can be dismantled demountable and recyclable structure and components and one that enables recycled and helps in the survival of the specialist and rare plants and fauna.'

THE ARGYLL MAUSOLEUM
KILMUN, ARGYLL AND BUTE

ICOSIS ARCHITECTS WITH STEVEN NEWSOM CONSERVATION ARCHITECT

The project safeguards the Category A listed Argyll Mausoleum, while providing both physical access to and interpretation of the Mausoleum, a wide variety of historically significant artefacts and the surrounding site, which includes a scheduled ancient monument and an adjacent Category A listed church. The rich heritage spread across a topographically challenging site in a remote location, the client's resources and their ability to sustainably manage the site in the long term all informed the brief and the strategic planning of the project.

Access to the mausoleum and the integration of the interpretation material has been delivered via a series of high quality, highly durable and low maintenance interpretation panels and carvings, along a route which leads visitors from an arrival and orientation shelter via an upgraded access to the Mausoleum. The interpretation materials are supplemented by a small reception and interpretation space within the church which provides a delivery point for information relating to the church.

By upgrading the amenity and performance of the church for its users, together with providing this education resource, a partnership between the custodians of these historically interlinked structures has been forged. Conservation of the Mausoleum itself included the sensitive repair of the unique cast iron dome, ensuring that the structure was made weathertight and the internal humidity regulated.

A Scottish Oak clad shelter gathers visitors, provides orientation and information, and acts as a 'signpost' for the site, as the Mausoleum is virtually hidden from the road. The route between the shelter and Mausoleum is formed from robust natural stone. The interventions overall provide a low key and economically sustainable solution.

The key to the design was a critical analysis of the client's initial brief, which sought a new-build visitor centre and cafe. Much time and effort was spent establishing the required level of intervention, the facilities appropriate to the heritage asset and then redefining the brief, removing the need for a new-build visitor centre. A focus was placed on delivering high quality but low key interventions, ones which are robust, easily maintained and managed, providing access and interpretation with minimal input.

The project's sustainability is fundamentally rooted in the critical resistance to build an unnecessary 'building'.

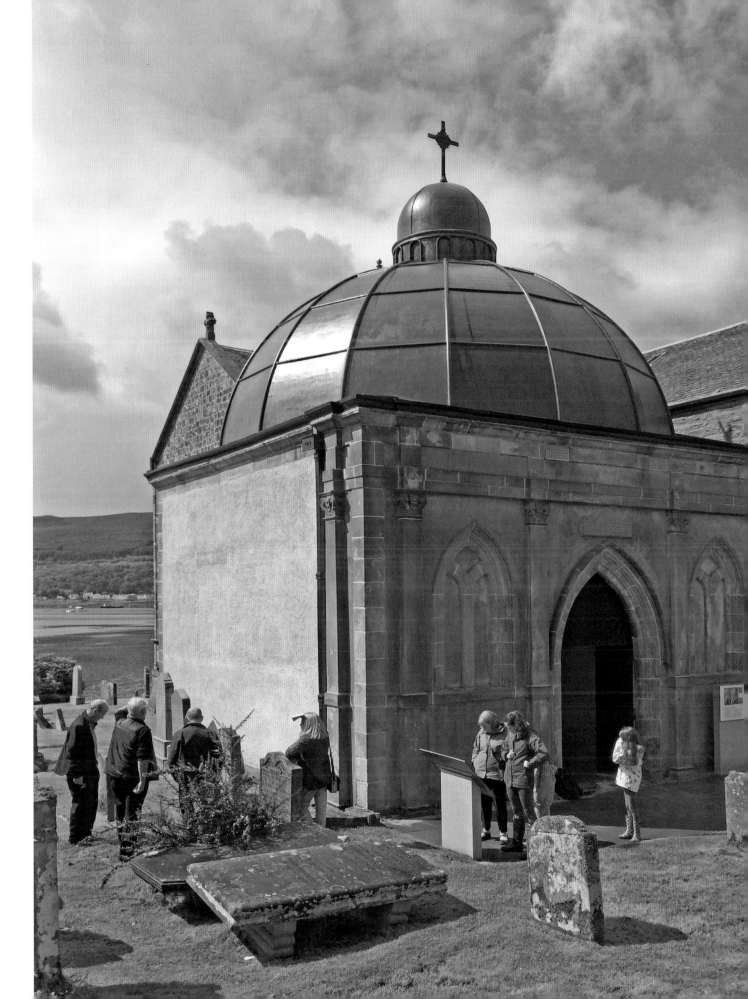

BIRKS CINEMA
ABERFLEDY

ROBIN BAKER ARCHITECTS

The Art Deco facade of Birks Cinema fronts a functional shed of roughcast rendered brick with pitched steel roof trusses with curved bottom chords. The original cinema housed 450 people in a largely unheated space.

The renovated building has a 100 seat auditorium and a double height cafe bar with two new large windows in the West elevation, allowing sun and daylight into the cafe and opening up views both in and out to the town square. Birks, being Scots for Birch trees, inspired a woodland theme for the interior design. The acoustic wall finishes in the auditorium represent an abstract woodland scene with tall, narrow panels with recessed vertical lights. A Birch woodland transfer and large letter Bs reminiscent of the original décor on the front doors double as a visual safety measure.

The refurbished cinema's energy performance exceed the then current Buildings Standards by approx 30% meeting the 2013 standards in advance. The building is very well insulated and is heated by a pair of 30kW gas boilers. There are heat recovery units in the auditorium and kitchen ventilation systems. Air conditioning is limited only to the highly sensitive projector enclosure and the control room. Underfloor cooling of the auditorium, during peak summer temperatures, is achieved by diverting the air supply through pipes encased in concrete below the floor.

Where there was a large derelict building, casting a shadow over Aberfeldy town centre, there is now a restored Art Deco cinema, which is a testament to the determined effort of Charlotte Flower and the community that she inspired.

The renovated Birks Cinema provides a key local focal point and is a source of entertainment and social activity. It has instilled a clear sense of change, an interest in and a sense of pride in Aberfeldy.

Birks Cinema; post and pre renovation

BUILDINGS AS AGENTS OF CHANGE

Raymond J Cole

The scale and pace of developments in the built environment over the past 50 years have been nothing other than phenomenal and have environmental impacts that are now of global consequence. The energy and resource use and associated greenhouse gas emissions associated with the construction and operation of buildings are acknowledged as a major cause of both global warming and environmental degradation. Indeed, green building design has been almost exclusively directed at reducing the degenerative consequences of the built environment on the health and integrity of ecological systems. Importantly, however, buildings offer the largest low cost potential carbon reductions in both developed and developing nations and will play a critical part of any global low carbon future. More broadly, buildings offer a powerful vehicle to engage public attention and nurture environmentally responsible attitudes and behaviours.

Buildings and human settlement patterns have historically expressed and made manifest the values and priorities of the societies that constructed them and changes to building practices signal a shift in these. Now, architectural approaches derived from the cultural and climatic uniqueness of the places where they are situated have been seriously eroded in a globalised culture. The debate regarding green building design has yet to acknowledge the potency of the overarching values and concerns that society holds or, indeed, how to harness them to effect positive change. A key question is, therefore, to what extent can buildings provide the role as agents of change to heighten society's recognition of environmental issues and responsibility to act?

A building as catalyst is typically understood as one that generates development in its immediate surroundings by increasing urban activity, economic benefit and stimulating new interrelationships within the public realm. Buildings embodying and expressing exemplary environmental performance and subsequently published through the professional press can inspire and motivate design professionals and their clients, increase the investor confidence and redefine regulatory frameworks, and thereby collectively both encouraging and enabling future green building development. While important, these perhaps still represent an insufficient view of the potential role that buildings and their supporting infrastructures can play.

If we accept that a building, in and of itself, cannot be sustainable but can be designed to support sustainable patterns of living, then the role the building plays is potentially of greater consequence than the building itself. Such a viewpoint is central to the emerging notion of regenerative development wherein, buildings, in addition to meeting their functional requirements, can assume a larger role and add other forms of 'value' to the community – improved social welfare, employment creation, new business opportunities, etc. Importantly, rather than reducing destructive impacts, regenerative approaches are directed to seeing buildings as enabling the full potential of the social and ecological systems in which they sit.

1. Ernest Sternberg, What makes buildings catalytic? How cultural facilities can be designed to spur surrounding development, *Journal of Architectural and Planning Research* 19:1 (Spring, 2002)

It would seem, therefore, that if buildings are to act as a catalyst for broader environmental change they must reestablish a meaningful connection to the places and communities in which they are situated. An important measure of their success relates to the manner and strength of this connection.

While the technical strategies of green design will remain valid, the intention, language and more comprehensive framing of regenerative development offers considerable potential to accelerate the development of systems-thinking, shared vision, shared ownership and shared responsibility. By offering a positive framing of environmental issues, regenerative approaches are inherently hopeful and full of promise – a marked contrast to the negative messaging of much of the current environmental discourse.

The notion of 'net-positive' propositions and approaches to building design practice has now emerged wherein some buildings may offer the potential of collecting more energy and water than they need to support their requirements. In doing so, it is not surprising that the primacy of the individual building as the focus of energy strategies is also being seriously challenged with an emerging tendency to view buildings as potential resource nodes within a networked infrastructure, such as a district energy system or smart grid network. Regenerative development also more effectively permits cross-scale, socio-ecological relationships and complex adaptive systems to frame approaches to building and infrastructure design.

Buildings clearly have consequence beyond those of importance to their owners and inhabitants or by offering new perspectives and possibilities to the broader design community and the overarching political, regulatory and financial institutions. Here, perhaps it is the processes of design and development that offer equal potency. Regenerative approaches emphasise the co-production of the built environment, greater equality between all stakeholders and demand more upfront time to discover what is valued. Consistent with Margaret Wheatley's notion that people care about what they create, forging partnerships and changing the power relationships inherent in the production of buildings provides greater assurance that the initial ambitions of a project are maintained through time.

Eventually perhaps, we will come to view the act of building not as destructive of natural systems and depleting the earth's resources but as contributing to and supporting the creation of a thriving, resilient and abundant world. To achieve such an ambition, we will need to articulate the vision and associated values necessary to affect and guide positive change and, in particular, be more considerate in how these are communicated to a broader public. Buildings, it would seem, can and should form a critical part of this communication process.

Raymond J Cole
University of British Columbia, Canada

WORK

NORTH WOODS TIMBER WORKSHOP
ULLAPOOL

NORTH WOODS CONSTRUCTION LTD

Based in a softwood plantation in the North West Highlands of Scotland, North Woods have been designing and constructing largely timber buildings for over 20 years. Many of these utilise homegrown timber, which can be milled and processed on site. In the last 10 years the company has expanded its capability into the use of cross-laminated timber (CLT) and evolved hybrid solutions to utilise both the best of modern off-site construction methods with the use of homegrown timber components.

Founded by an ecologist with 40 years experience of environmental management and construction, the company has always been guided by a strong set of ecological principles which its new workshops naturally epitomise.

To achieve an efficient and long-lasting structural envelope with timber sourced from Europe's most ecologically managed plantations, North Woods collaborated with Eurban Ltd to design and procure a Sitka Spruce glulam frame which is wrapped in a mixed softwood envelope of thin CLT.

With frames on 6m centres, the purlins are designed to accommodate the depth of a local straw bale of which 550 were used to insulate the roof. Walls were then framed on the outside of the CLT with softwood from the surrounding plantation and insulated with sheep's wool. They are clad with a rainscreen of painted Sitka Spruce felled and processed on site from the surrounding forest. The building is used to process timber from the surrounding plantation using an electric bandsaw mill. It can then be kiln dried, resawn and dressed on the premises to make anything required for North Woods' projects, which range from post and beam frames to furniture. Whilst whole houses are designed and built by the company, the new facility has been designed to focus on off-site construction of cabins, huts and high quality building components.

The workshop, the plantation it is sited within and the families that make up the workforce all live on site in self built cabins, adding up to an unusually integrated and ecologically defined lifestyle and work ethic.

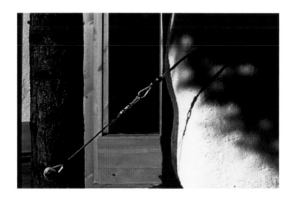

STRAW BALE OFFICE
DUNNING, PERTHSHIRE

GAIA ARCHITECTS

The client, an architect and member of the UK Sustainable Construction Forum, decided to build an office in the garden and approached Gaia Architects in the expectation of achieving a truly sustainable building with a healthy indoor climate. With a desire to be as sustainable as possible, the client was happy to support an experimental approach.

Starting life as a demonstration of a moisture transfusive wall, discussions soon led to development of a more ambitious agenda. It provided Gaia with the opportunity to innovate based on their recent research into 'Adding Value to Timber in the Northern Periphery' a collaboration with Finnish and Norwegian partners. Hence locally sourced Larch roundpole was identified as available to form the frame and a local materials audit led to the investigation of the potential of straw bale walls.

The project then developed using almost entirely local, natural and reclaimed materials sourced from within 20 miles.

The 30m^2 building features a curved glulam roof on eight poles braced with stainless steel shipping fixings. None of the timber is treated, and it is properly and finely detailed so that all areas, such as the raised floor platform, receive adequate ventilation to prevent deterioration. The building is unheated.

Materials include straw bale walls rendered on both sides in lime plaster and limewash, sharpened hazel twigs, clay-straw mix filling, reclaimed Douglas Fir floorboards, reclaimed wood wool insulation, reclaimed window casements from a demolished shed and even an 'as found' gas pipe offcut that serves as a porthole window. The untreated sheep's wool insulated roof was covered with turf from the garden to replace the displaced garden space.

Radical innovation on a small building, with a willing client/user, was probably easier and more acceptable than it might be on a larger scale, where the users might be unknown and difficult to wrap into understanding the ongoing implications.

SIMPLE MINDS RECORDING STUDIO
LOCH EARN, STIRLINGSHIRE

GAIA ARCHITECTS

This is an example of high-tech design enclosed in benign materials and with both the thermal and acoustic performance specification at the highest level. The scheme consists of a double hexagonal plan, with acoustic requirements that avoided parallel surfaces in order to accurately control reverberation.

The studio space is double-height with glulam portal frames and – unusually for a recording studio – glazing to afford views across the loch. On the roof are two weathervanes, one spelling out 'Simple' and the other 'Minds'.

The building, completed in 1986, was used as the major base for much of the band's recording over a 10-year period and was the inspiration behind their 1989 single 'This is Your Land' that urges us to take care of the world we live in before it's too late. It was also designed with future flexibility in mind. In 2000 Gaia were commissioned by the new owner of the estate to convert the studio into a house.

The studio now has two en-suite double bedrooms, and additional accommodation centred on an open-plan living space with a galleried landing above, which opens onto a covered balcony.

Norton Park demonstrates that the cultural and social significance of heritage buildings need not be sacrificed in order to deliver economically and environmentally sustainable projects.

NORTON PARK REFURBISHMENT
EDINBURGH

BURNETT POLLOCK ASSOCIATES

The Albion Trust commissioned Burnett Pollock Associates to convert and refurbish Norton Park to provide high quality colocation office space for charities in Scotland's capital. The challenging brief was to create useable, accessible offices while minimising environmental impact within a realistic budget.

Norton Park is typical of schools built at the turn of the 20th century. The building had advantages, such as cultural significance and low embodied energy and toxicity. It also had challenges, such as a redundant use, poor insulation, outmoded and inefficient services common of traditional stone walled and slate roofed pre-1919 construction in Scotland. Carfrae's original design was recognised by its protection as a Category B listed building and this was crucial, in both saving Norton Park and in raising project funds. The eventual project cost was considered to be around 75% of that of a comparable new building, excluding land value.

Best conservation practice was followed to retain and repair fabric, incorporating new materials only where required, which like the original construction were hygroscopic, allowing moisture to move through the building structure. Many features of the building were retained or reused, such as internal doors, ironmongery and decorative tiling, retaining the cultural identity.

A hierarchy of material use, for new interventions, of FSC certified timber, steel and glass was adopted with bolted fixings to ensure ease of future reuse or recycling. Finishes use low toxicity materials for floor coverings and decoration. All construction waste was separated for recycling. The performance of the external fabric of the building was improved with the introduction of insulation and high performance secondary windows and a comprehensive program of services included:

- multi-zoned condensing boilers
- background ventilation with heat recovery and passive slate pre-heat
- high efficiency lighting with presence detection
- gravity feed rainwater harvesting tank
- door hold-open devices and Braille encrypted / voiced lift to maximise accessibility

Norton Park has outperformed both the original brief and most new contemporary offices. Monitoring studies show that it is liked by its users and has an exceptionally low void rate. The additional cost of improving the building performance, beyond that required by the building codes at the time, delivered a two-thirds reduction in CO_2 emissions and energy costs, with a payback period estimated at 10–12 years.

SCOTSTOUN HOUSE REFURBISHMENT
SOUTH QUEENSFERRY

HAA DESIGN / ARUP GROUP LTD

Ove Arup & Partners, as the firm were then known, first began to practise in Edinburgh in 1960. Over the next few years its local staff numbers increased, until they occupied several small offices in the centre of the city. It was clearly desirable that all should be housed in a single location, and so the firm's own integrated practice, Arup Associates, was commissioned to design a new purpose-built office. This was a low, single level structure within the walled garden of a previously demolished country house, in the grounds of a 2.43ha estate at South Queensferry, 8km West of Edinburgh.

By the early 2000s, the original building had started to show the limitations of its 1960s technology, and was also becoming a constraint on the way Arup wanted to work. A development plan was therefore prepared to bring new life into it, and provide a contemporary environment to suit the firm's needs now and into the future.

The original building had been Category B listed by Historic Scotland in October 2005. This introduced significant challenges with regard to achieving the desired BREEAM Excellent rating, and the development therefore became a detailed balance between preserving the qualities of Scotstoun House and meeting the needs of a 21st century office building. This involved maximising the original building as a working space and complementing this with a new extension containing support functions. The link between old and new created a useful intermediate zone for breakout, group working, and informal interaction.

The project consisted of the refurbishment and extension of the office, which is set within its own parkland site. The new build aspect of the project occupies the Eastern side of the walled garden, maximising solar gain and properly engaging with the garden environment. A glass link sensitively connects new to old, preserving the original design and enhancing the new build. The main office area has been designed to cater for 140 workstations, based on the Kinnarps bench arrangement. The grounds within the walled garden have been enhanced to allow a piazza circulation area with bench seats. The project achieved a BREEAM Excellent rating, low carbon building energy performance with use of a biomass boiler, sustainable urban drainage and on-site recycled waste storage.

GREAT GLEN HOUSE
INVERNESS

ROBERTSON DEVELOPMENTS | KEPPIE DESIGN

Great Glen House, the headquarters for Scottish Natural Heritage, was procured via a design competition and won by Robertson Developments and Keppie Design in 2004.

The ultra low carbon design uses entirely A rated materials and employs night cooling and passive air management using the 90m long three-storey atrium as the air management engine for the largely open plan offices. The client brief was very demanding and achieving this required the design team to develop components of the building from first principles according to building physics, as products with the required performance were commercially unavailable. Many building elements, such as frequency selective acoustic wall linings and thermal-acoustic ceiling rafts, containing services, needed to be bespoke to provide the standards of performance and BREEAM accreditation required.

Great Glen House has an airtightness of $4.87\text{m}^3/\text{m}^2/$ hour @50Pa, and scored the highest ever BREEAM score then awarded of 84.01%. Water consumption per occupant is only 0.99m^3 compared to a best practice figure of 6.4m^3. The exterior is clad in 300 tons of local Larch, felled and sawn in line with a specification developed to suit the building and setting. The project budget was £12m. Equivalent at the time to a comparable speculative office building and it was designed and delivered in 18 months.

Great Glen House was modelled using TAS software, which guided development of the envelope and provided confidence in the passive design. Internal monitoring stations and external weather stations, in combination with the Building Management System, enables fine-tuning of the building in response to daily climate variation. Performance generally met predictions, with a 17-week heating season and a carbon footprint of 8.4Kg/m^2, while ongoing monitoring demonstrates that, 10 years later, it continues to perform well.

Great Glen House won the BCO corporate workplace of the year award, demonstrating that sustainability doesn't necessarily require any compromise in function or joy.

NEW OFFICES FOR RUSSWOOD LTD
NEWTONMORE

HRI ARCHITECTS

Russwood Ltd have built a reputation for supplying high quality responsibly sourced timber products throughout Scotland. The company is a major employer in the village of Newtonmore in the Cairngorms National Park and recognises that it has a responsibility to both the local community and economy.

Russwood decided to work with nature long before it became fashionable and they supply FSC and PEFC sourced materials, which require the management of the environment, rather than its exploitation. To achieve environmental improvement throughout its operations, Russwood is committed to establishing an Environmental Management System to meet the requirements of the international standard ISO 14001:2004, and set environmental objectives and targets which are regularly reviewed and revised.

It followed that when the need arose for a new office building, the company recognised the opportunity to have a building designed and built that created a working environment that would promote togetherness as well as efficiency. The design needed to recognise the importance and value of the location and the materials that would form the building.

Spaces were carefully considered to allow good communication, but also provide privacy when needed. Facilities are shared where possible and the design allows for future expansion.

The form and external appearance of the building make direct reference to the landscape. A large shallow pitched roof with an upturn at the entrance mimics the rolling hills, and the colours reflect the shades of both sky and hills through the seasons, connecting the building with its setting.

The building is oriented to benefit from solar heat gain, it is highly insulated and utilises natural ventilation. The heating system is biomass, fuelled by the waste timber offcuts from the sawmill, squeezing the last bit of benefit out of the company's raw materials.

Maximising the use of locally supplied materials and labour reduced both embodied and transport energy and made sure as much of the financial investing as possible stayed in the local economy and contributed to a sense of community. All the natural materials used have low VOCs and toxic materials were largely avoided.

The new office building is a major investment for the company, in people, in the community and in the future, as it responds to the local and wider environment in a responsible manner.

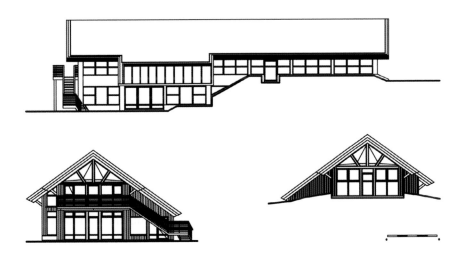

NATURAL POWER OFFICE DEVELOPMENT
FORREST ESTATE, DUMFRIES & GALLOWAY

MAKAR

The Forrest Estate in Galloway is one of the largest private woodlands in Scotland. It is owned by Fred Olsen Ltd, which is also the owner of Natural Power – a renewable energy consultancy business.

In 1999, the Estate commissioned Neil Sutherland to design a 'comfortable, healthy and bright office space' to be built on Forrest Estate ground. The building was designed to accommodate up to 20 people based on a hot-desking working principle. The building extends to 360m² over two floors.

A key aim of the brief was to make the building as sustainable as possible and to show that renewables and sustainable design make long-term commercial sense. This approach included using timber sourced directly from the Forrest Estate, which make up ²/3 of the timber used. This timber includes the large section heartwood Douglas Fir used for the principal frame with exposed post, beam and trusses.

The building sits on a hillock, set back from trees and laid out on an East West orientation to maximise solar gain along the glazed South face. The office is earth sheltered and built into the hill at the East, providing level access to the first floor. It is completely free of external utilities provision – using local hydropower from the Estate's own hydro scheme, ground water from a borehole and foul water is drained to a septic tank. Solar hot water panels provide hot water. Double glazing using low emissivity glass is fitted throughout the building.

Good solar orientation provides good natural daylighting, and generous roof overhangs provide glare control. The 150mm thick turf for the roof was stripped from the building site and the adjacent hill. Sawmill waste was used for path materials and mulch, and locally quarried stone was used as the base material in the construction of the car park.

This office building sequestrated high levels of embodied carbon during construction, and uses 70% less energy than an equivalent sized conventional contemporary building.

The completed building remains a physical embodiment of Natural Power's brand image and belief in sustainability and renewable energy.

THE ECOLOGY CENTRE
KINGHORN, FIFE

STUART HANNAH, ADD ARCHITECTS

The Ecology Centre is a successful local charity that provides environmental education, volunteering and conservation activities that benefit both people and the environment.

The project brief was to provide space for daily activities, a building that would sit quietly in the landscape and that would also follow ecological principles – maximising energy efficiency and the use of natural, recycled or recyclable materials. These objectives were achieved with a building designed by local architect Stuart Hannah. The long, low profile of the building takes its architectural reference from a nearby boathouse. The building sits well on the lochside nestled among surrounding hills – a natural appearance is achieved using Scottish Larch cladding and a green sedum roof.

A conscious decision was made to adopt a fabric first approach to energy efficiency on the main building, maximising airtightness and thermal performance while keeping a tight rein on costs. The building used the Beattie Passivhaus accredited system of a timber-frame build with high performance insulation and triple glazing. This achieved an airtightness of $0.16m^3/m^2/hr$ @50Pascal, contributing to an A rated Energy Performance Certificate. The building incorporates photovoltaic panels to generate electricity, a solar hot water system and mechanical ventilation heat recovery to minimise energy use.

Workshop and storage space has been created to the rear of the building by converting 7 old shipping containers. A courtyard space between the main building and the containers provides a covered walkway, on the roof of which are mounted the solar panels.

Personality has been added with a mosaic of recycled glass and ceramics made by staff and volunteers, cycle racks of Oak logs made by a local social enterprise and ornamental gates designed by staff and made by a local blacksmith. Volunteers played an active role throughout the build process.

The building perfectly accommodates the activities run by the Centre and enables the principles of energy efficiency, use of natural materials and recycling to be demonstrated and shared.

KNOCKANDO WOOLMILL
KNOCKANDO, ABERLOUR

LDN ARCHITECTS

LDN Architects had to look no further than the traditional timber structure and cladding of the original mill, byre and shop at Knockando Woolmill for encouragement and inspiration to use timber as the predominant material for the project. At over 200 years old, and much altered, the original timber had already proven to be fit for purpose, durable, flexible and capable of adaptation to suit new uses.

Parts of the timber structures had become extremely fragile however, mostly due to under-investment and lack of maintenance, and careful repair strategies had to be devised in line with the conservation policies and principles of minimum intervention adopted on the project.

As much as possible of the original Larch vertical cladding boards and cover pieces were salvaged and repaired for reuse. Where necessary, new Scottish Larch cladding boards and cover pieces were introduced, salvaged and repaired for reuse.

Timber was the obvious choice of construction material for the new conservation training workshop. It has timber framed walls, glulam columns and beams and bespoke roof trusses made from locally sourced stress graded timber. Sheeps wool insulation is incorporated in the construction. In harmony with the original buildings, the new workshop is clad with vertical Scottish Larch.

The timber detailing on all of the buildings was carefully designed and executed by skilled local joiners. Examples are the pitch Pine wall and ceiling linings in the mill shop, the broad Pine flooring in the mill and millhouse and the repairs to, and replacement of, numerous components, such as traditional sash and case windows and lined doors.

BUTE RECYCLING CENTRE
ROTHESAY ISLE OF BUTE

COLLECTIVE ARCHITECTURE

The brief for the Recycling Centre was developed by Fyne Homes in conjunction with Bute Waste Watchers. From the start there was an explicit requirement to utilise sustainable methods of building, design and material sourcing. The Centre has provided Bute Waste Watchers with a firm base for their strategy to promote and develop recycling activities on the mainland as well as the Island of Bute. Operating in Rothesay, the group make up a significant part of a movement in the Argyll and Bute area, which has seen the highest levels of household recycling in Scotland in recent years. The Centre has been developed with the understanding that for recycling to truly flourish within the community it has to be seen and understood as part of an important and normal process.

The majority of material used to construct the Centre was recycled, reclaimed or supplied from sustainable sources. The timber cladding is local Larch. The bricks are quality seconds, which may normally have been scrapped, but were suitable for use in this case as an external cladding material and used with the injunction, 'never to let two bricks the same touch'. Short supply brick styles resulted in the vibrant mix of colours visible all around the building. The roof is 100% recycled aluminium, made of exactly the

same aluminium cans that the Centre itself collects, crushes and sells on to maintain viability.

Recycled glazed screens are used throughout the building, constructed from broken bottles sourced from the island and constructed by a Glasgow artist in collaboration with Haran Glass. They act to filter coloured light through the building, an effect that changes throughout the day and differs from week to week and season to season. Throughout the interior, recycled and reclaimed elements have been incorporated, sourced by the architect and contractor from neglected stores around the Island. Both the kitchen and bathroom are constructed entirely from found objects. All doors were retrieved from buildings due to be demolished and, where necessary, treated to achieve required standards.

Bute Waste Watchers is a successful business, exporting compacted pallets of aluminium, plastic and textiles throughout the UK. Through their recycling activities and by harnessing the symbolic qualities of the Centre, they continue to promote and communicate the issues of recycling and sustainability throughout Bute.

TONGLAND POWER STATION
DUMFRIES AND GALLOWAY

SIR ALEXANDER GIBB & PARTNERS

Tongland power station was built as the control station of the highly influential Galloway hydroelectric power scheme completed in 1936. Hydroelectric power (HEP), developed sensitively, is a non-polluting source of electricity that helps decrease dependence on fossil fuels.

The Galloway scheme was the first required by parliament to satisfy an 'amenity' clause ensuring the structures' appearance respected their setting in the Galloway hills. Harnessing run-of-the-river technology, it removed the need for entirely man-made reservoirs, and allowed the natural course of the landscape to provide a head of water. Its dams incorporated innovative fish passes to ameliorate the impact of such industry on the aquatic and riparian systems. The high standards of environmental performance are set, including preserving the quality of the water, the landscape and its wildlife, and managed in 2016 through a biodiversity action plan.

It was the arrival of aluminium smelting in the Scottish Highlands and consequent demand for power on a large scale that made the development of HEP feasible. The Galloway scheme was pioneering as the first integrated and complex system

predating the 1943 Hydro Electric Act. By 2008, approximately a century after the industry began, hydroelectric now provides 12% of the gross power consumed in the UK.

Developing HEP in Galloway was first mooted in 1923 but the agrarian nature of the region meant that it could not provide an income sufficient to be viable. It was not until the arrival in 1933 of the national grid, enabling the power to be transmitted to the central belt and North West England, that the problem was resolved.

Tongland Power Station is a modern classical landmark, the lowest and largest of those in the Galloway Scheme. The rectangular pilastered concrete turbine hall, with a handsome interior containing three turbines, is accompanied by a circular plan surge tower of riveted steel set on reinforced concrete arches and a diminutive rectangular valve house. Water is supplied from a reservoir contained by a concrete arch and granite dam with monumental flood gates.

The success of the Galloway and Lanark HEP schemes laid the foundations for the nationalisation of this sustainable industry.

CIRCULAR ECONOMY
David Cheshire

Using salvaged and reclaimed materials is a long tradition stretching back centuries, but is increasingly difficult with the rise of complex components, the easy access to new products and the demise of the salvage industry. Looking at the beautiful, inspiring buildings in this book, it is hard to imagine that one day they will be demolished, but history shows that very few endure. So, to be truly sustainable, we have to think about not only the first life of the building, but of its next life and the future of its hard-won materials and components.

Despite the efforts of some designers, we are locked into a 'linear economy' model, where materials are won, processed, manufactured, used and then thrown away. Our buildings are demolished before their time and are stripped out with alarming frequency, leaving waste that can only be 'downcycled' into lower grade products. For example, solid timber is chipped or burnt, structural concrete becomes nonstructural aggregate and even modular, potentially reusable units like bricks are often crushed rather than reclaimed. Given that the built environment demands around 40% of the world's extracted materials and demolition waste represents the largest waste stream in many countries, this seems a highly wasteful approach. Surely we can do better. This brings us to the idea of a circular economy where, inspired by nature, waste from one system becomes a resource for another and the value of these resources is retained in perpetuity.

For buildings, this means creating a regenerative built environment that prioritises retention and refurbishment over demolition and rebuilding. It means designing buildings that can be adapted, reconstructed and deconstructed to extend their life and that allow components and materials to be salvaged for reuse or recycling.

New business models allow shortlived elements of the building to be leased instead of purchased, providing occupants with increased flexibility and the ability to procure a service rather than having the burden of ownership. Building collaborative relationships enables manufacturers to invest in product development instead of having to focus on the next sale. Creating a demand for reclaimed or remanufactured components will stimulate the local economy and create new industries, while reducing waste.

A forensic examination of the materials that go into buildings ensures that any potentially harmful substances are purged from the design. This improves internal air quality as well as allowing biological materials to be returned safely to the biosphere.

Of course, creating a circular building while still locked into a linear economy means designers have to swim against the tide, but there are some positive signs of change. Scotland has joined other countries such as Japan and the Netherlands in developing circular economy policies and is promoting the transition to a more circular economy by promoting remanufacturing, producer responsibility and durable products. It is also prioritising construction and the built environment as one of 4 areas of focus.

Applying circular economy thinking to the construction industry is not straightforward. Buildings are made from thousands of components with a widely varying life ranging from the structure and foundations that may be around for hundreds of years, to the interior fixtures and fittings that may be gone in 2 or 3 years. In my book, *Building Revolutions*, I propose some design principles for circular economy buildings. An underpinning principle is that of 'designing in layers', as proposed by the writer Stewart Brand and architect Frank Duffy. This approach considers each of the major components of the building to be separate and independent, comprising the structure, the skin, the services, the space plan and the stuff. The structure is the longest lasting and is independent of the skin (the façade and roof); the services are an accessible layer that can be replaced as required and the space plan and the stuff describe the shortlived elements that can be reconfigured and changed regularly.

It is easier to imagine how a more circular approach could be taken to these inner layers: interiors could be designed to accommodate their shorter lifespans by using modular systems that can be reconfigured; or elements could be leased instead of purchased to allow them to be returned for reuse or remanufacture. But this still leaves the question of how to deal with the longer-life elements, the structure and the fabric of the building. Should they be designed as robust, adaptable structures that can endure, even when this may demand additional resources, or should we acknowledge the short lifespan of many buildings and design for disassembly and reuse?

The answer is more nuanced than simply choosing one route or the other. Although it may initially seem contradictory, designing for deconstruction can actually help to make a building more robust and adaptable as its components can be separated more easily and different elements made more accessible for repair or replacement.

But it is not enough to design for disassembly, as there still needs to be a market for the components at the end of their first life. Creating a market for salvaged stock means that reused components have to be as readily available, attractive and as fully certified as new products. There has to be new fiscal incentives and policy initiatives to drive this new economic model.

A project that was developed during the UK Green Building Council Future Leaders programme proposed an interesting solution that may help to drive change: an online hub to create a marketplace for building materials. The hub would document the materials used in the building and make the information accessible to interested parties. The materials would be documented in a materials passport which would contain a quantified list of construction materials and modular elements along with their recovery rating.

The hub would allow users to find out when materials are available and place bids on them. It could help to assign a value to materials held within existing buildings, with interested parties being able to purchase an interest in the material in advance of it being salvaged from the building. This initiative has now been developed into a start-up company, called LOOP (http://loop-hub.co.uk/) that aims to make the reuse of materials quick, easy and commercially viable.

An approach that applies the principles of 'design for disassembly' and 'building in layers' enables buildings to be reconfigured for different uses: façades can be replaced without affecting the structure, atria and stairwells can be created, and new interiors can be implemented. Applying the principles of disassembly allows a building to be more adaptable and can give it a longer life. And of course, if the building is overwhelmed by the future and is earmarked for demolition, then it can be disassembled and the components can be reclaimed for reuse, remanufacture or recycling, even providing a positive residual value at its end of life. Perhaps the idea should be that buildings endow future generations with the precious resources that they will need to live their lives and buildings are therefore designed to endure, either in whole or in part.

David Cheshire
Regional Director at AECOM

Richard Atkins
DIP ARCH (Edin), RIBA, FRIAS

Richard is a practising architect and holds the Advanced Accredited in Sustainability from the Royal Incorporation of Architects in Scotland (RIAS), as well as being Scotland's first Certifier of Design (Section 6 – Energy). He has been responsible for a number of innovative, environmentally responsible and award-winning projects that demonstrate that not only are high design quality and a sustainable built environment achievable, but that it makes sound economic and social sense. A past Chair of the Scottish Ecological Design Association, Richard has advised, amongst others, the RIAS, the Scottish Government and Historic Environment Scotland and at the time of publication is completing a PhD in the Assessment of Sustainability in the Existing Built Environment at Glasgow Caledonian University and co-authored *The Sustainability Guide to the Plan of Work* 2013 (2016).

Chris Butters

A Norwegian citizen, holds a BA in Literature (Stellenbosch), a Masters in Architecture (Montpellier) and a Diploma in Energy Planning (Oslo). He has worked with architecture, energy, ecology and sustainable planning for 35 years, as practising architect, author, lecturer and international consultant. He is the author or co-author of eight books. Formerly director of Norwegian Architects for Sustainable Development and consultant at the Ideas Bank Foundation. More recently, Chris has been researcher at Warwick University, UK. He leads a postgraduate programme on Energy and Sustainable Development at Oslo University. Chris worked for 10 years in Bhutan as architect and project coordinator for schools and a hospital, as well as doing Tibetological research. He is a co-founder of the GAIA group in Norway (1982) and GAIA International (1992), a pioneering network for sustainable building and 'deep green' solutions. He is also the creator of the Sustainability Value Map.

Carlo R. Campos
Architect

Carlos is an architect from Spain with a serious commitment for minimising the environmental impact from the construction sector. He is concerned about the different sustainability assessment methods within the built environment.BREEAM qualified assessor for new construction and existing buildings in UK and internationally, Carlos is completing his PhD studies in Simplified Life Cycle Assessment Methodology for new and existing buildings at Strathclyde University of Glasgow combining his research with casual work as technical consultant and lecturer assistant at the Architecture department.

David Cheshire
AECOM
MSc BSc(Hons) MEI MIEMA CEnv ACIBSE BREEAM AP

David Cheshire is a Regional Director at AECOM and the author of *Building Revolutions*, a RIBA Publication that explains how to apply circular economy to the built environment. The book includes illustrative methods and examples of how circular economy principles can be applied to the built environment.

Ray Cole
PhD, University of Wales
BSc, City University, London

Ray is a former director of the School of Architecture and Landscape Architecture, where he has been teaching environmental issues in building design for over 35 years. His current research interests relate to regenerative design, building environmental performance assessment, and human and automated intelligence. Ray was selected as a North American Association of Collegiate Schools of Architecture Distinguished Professor for 'sustained commitment to building environmental research and teaching' in 2001. In 2003, he received the US Green Building Council's Green Public Service Leadership Award. Ray was the recipient of the 2008 Sustainable Buildings Canada Life-Time Achievement Award and the 2009 Canada Green Building Council's Life-Time Leadership Award. He is a past director of the Canadian Green Building Council, an honorary member of the Architectural Institute of BC, Fellow of the Royal Architectural Institute of Canada, and holds the UBC designation of Distinguished University Scholar.

Professor Sandy Liddell Halliday
BSc(Hons) MPhil CEng MCIBSE FRSA
Principal, Gaia Research

Sandy is a chartered engineer and Principal of Gaia Research, which she founded (1995) to develop sustainable solutions for the built environment. Sandy's first degree in Engineering Design and Appropriate Technology (1982–1985) focused on socially and environmentally responsible engineering. She initially worked in the design of socially useful products and moved into the building sector as a research manager to develop and disseminate information on passive design, resource efficient and clean technologies, healthy buildings, and benign construction processes, products and materials. She is a specialist advisor for clients, architectural and engineering practices, offering real time guidance on strategies for achieving affordable sustainable buildings and places at all stages from briefing and specification to tendering, handover, operation and post-occupancy evaluation. Her work extends to research, policy, brief development, community consultation, inter-disciplinary education and development of tools to support design and delivery. She was Visiting Professor of Engineering Design for Sustainable Development in the School of Architecture, University of Strathclyde until 2008 and is now Visiting Lecturer Energy, Environment and Sustainable Development – Oslo International Summer School. Her practical experience is well documented in research publications and in her *Code of Practice for Buildings & their Services* (1994), *The Green Guide to the Architects Job Book* (1999), *Sustainable Construction* (2008) *and The Sustainability Guide to the Plan of Work 2013* (2016).

Jim Johnson

An architect for well over 50 years and member of SEDA since its foundation in 1991, Jim worked in Cumbernauld New Town, moved into housing regeneration in the 1970/80s whilst in the Dept. of Architecture at Strathclyde University. Co – founder of the University's ASSIST project, which pioneered a conservation led approach to urban regeneration. Tenement flats repaired and upgraded under the control of locally based housing associations, keeping community life and local networks intact. He applied the same principles in the Edinburgh Old Town Renewal Trust from 1986–1995 and later worked in Eastern European historic towns as a consultant to UNESCO. Jim is co-author of *Renewing Old Edinburgh: The enduring legacy of Patrick Geddes*, 2010.

Emily Stephen
MArch, MA(Sociology)

Emily has a background in Architecture and in Sociology. She has participated, worked and taught on self build projects across Scotland, including helping to establish the SEDA Construction School, SEDA Build, in 2014. Emily spent several years working with Roots Architecture, focusing on rural projects across the West Coast of Scotland before setting up Nor, a design studio based in Glasgow.

Chris Stewart
B'Arch(hons), Dip Arch, ARB, RIAS, RIBA

Following international success in Edinburgh, London and Berlin, Chris Stewart Architects were formed in May 1997 to pursue the themes of participation and sustainability in architecture. Chris Stewart Architects for ten years were recognised with various national and international awards. In May 2007 Chris transferred company ownership from himself to an employee owned trust which together with his work colleagues formed Collective Architecture. Their work has been widely published and exhibited in Glasgow, London, Barcelona, Chicago and at the Venice Biennale. Collective Architecture are based in Glasgow, however, have recently opened a new office in Edinburgh and are working on a number of major commissions across the UK. With over 25 years' experience of practicing architecture, Chris is an RIAS Sustainability Accredited Architect, an RIAS Sustainability Assessor, the current Chair/ Director of the Scottish Ecological Design Association, the current Chair of the Deconstruction Group (CSIC / Zero Waste Scotland) and was a member of the RIAS Council from 2012 to 2016. Chris leads a design unit at Strathclyde University, is an external examiner at the University of Edinburgh and has taught at a number of Schools of Architecture including Aberdeen, Lille and the Mackintosh School of Architecture.

Lotte Glob House & Studio; Andrew Lee and Gokay Deveci

Plummerswood; Micheal Wolchover, Sandy Halliday

Timber House; John Gilbert Architects

Two Detached Houses at Comrie; Jennifer Macleay and Colin Henderson

New Eco House; Simpson & Brown

The Houl; Simon Winstanley

Model D House; Stuart Johnstone

Edenhope; Sarah Eno and Andy Swales

Kincraig Milehouse; David Somerville Architects

2 Semi-Detached Houses; Colin Henderson

The Bourne House; Howard Liddell

Japanese House; Alan Craigie

Suburban Passive House; Douglas Gibb Photography

The Stonehouses; Stuart Bashaw and Leila Bagshaw

Signal Station House; Torquil Cramer

Ellieside Cottage; Nick Brown

Refurbishment of 11 Annat Road; Historic Scotland

Scotstarvit Tower Cottage; National Trust Scotland, Historic Environment Scotland

Mains of Branshogle; Angus Bremmer Photography

The Rings; David Barbour

Ramp House; David Barbour

Homes For The Future; Roan Rutherford

East Whins; Tom Manley Photography and 3 sketches by Gillies MacPhail

The 'Tigh-Na-Claddach'; Andrew Lee

Dormont Passivhaus Development; Dormont Estate

Slateford Green; Photographs: John Reiach . Sketch: Hackland and Dore Architects

Glenalmond Street; Colin Gray Photography

A'Chrannag; Andrew Lee and Gokay Deveci

Archers hall; Paul Zanre

Commonwealth Games Athletes Village; Michael Gray

PHOTOGRAPHY & IMAGE CREDITS

Macrae Housing; John Reiach

Inter War Public Housing; John Reiach

Edinburgh Colonies; David Seel

Fairfield Housing; Gaia Architects

9–11 Gilmours Close; Assist Architects

James Nisbet Street; Assist Architects

Nicolson Street Housing; Gaia Architects

New Lanark; New Lanark Trust

Acharacle Primary School; Gaia Architects

Notre Dame Primary School; Greg Piechowicz

Colmonell Primary School; Gordon Fleming

RBGE Lecture Theatre; Michael Wolchover and Smith Scott Mullan Associates

Edinburgh Centre for Carbon Innovation (ECCI); Dave Morris

Low Carbon Technology Building; Angus J Allan

Portsoy Boat Building Centre; Nigel Rigden

The Boiler House; Andrew Lee Photography

The Big Shed; Sue Manning, Marieke McBean

Grassmarket Community Project; Gillian Hayes at Dapple Photography

The Noust; Sebb Hathaway and Neil Boyd

Wikihouse; Phil Wilkinson and Akiko Kobayashi

Love Milton; Stuart Rennie and Emily Stephen

David Douglas Pavilion; Robin Baker Architects

Reidvale Steet-Scaping & Urban Allotments; Assist Design

T.R.E.E Centre; Marcin Szczepanski

Business Centre for the Galson Estate Trust; Chris Morgan; Photographs taken whilst with Locate Architects, Chris is now with John Gilbert Architects

Land Sea and Islands Centre Refurbishment; Sam Foster and Alison and Gordon Stewart

Woodschool Compost Toilet; Chris Morgan; Photographs taken whilst with Locate Architects, Chris is now with John Gilbert Architects

GALE Forum Visitor Centre; Jennifer Macleay and Colin Henderson

The Shields Centre; Keith Hunter Photography

Girvan Community Hospital; Keith Hunter Photography

Centre of Integrated Care; Macmon, Mike Bolan and Jane Kelly

Royal Commonwealth Pool Refurbishment; BuroHappold Engineering

McLaren Community Leisure Centre; Gaia Architects

Glentress Visitor Centre Masterplan; Michael Wolchover

Loch Leven Heritage Trail; Icosis Architects and Sean Begley

Arbroath Abbey Visitor Reception Building; Keith Hunter Photography

Abbotsford Visitor Reception Building; Paul Zanre

Loch Lomond Park Centre; Keith Hunter Photography and Dallman Johnstone

Glencoe Visitor Centre; Gaia Architects

Trossachs Discovery Centre; Keith Hunter Photography and Dallman Johnstone

Scottish Storytelling Centre; BrendanMacNeill and Malcolm Fraser Architects

Waterston House; Simpson & Brown and Torquil Cramer

Forsinard Lookout Tower; Sjoerd Tel

Alpine House; Michael Wolchover for Smith Scott Mullan Associates

The Argyll Mausoleum; Icosis Architects

Birks Cinema; Robin Baker Architects

North Woods Timber Workshop; Bernard Planterose

Straw Bale Office; Gaia Architects

Simple Minds Recording Studio; Gaia Architects

Norton Park Refurbishment; Burnett Pollock Associates

Great Glen House: Headquarters of SNH; Michael Wolchover

New offices for Russwood Ltd.; Mark Williams and Ewen Weatherspoon

Natural Power Office Development; Ted Leeming and Peter Devlin

The Ecology Centre; Alison Crook

Knockando Woolmill; LDN Architects

Bute Recycling Centre; Andrew Lee Photography

Tongland Power Station; Tom Jeffs (CC) and Scottish Power

SPONSORS

With special thanks for their sponsorship and support:

Anderson Bell Christie

Arup Scotland

Brennan & Wilson Architects

Dallman Johnstone

Dormont Estate

Gaia Architects

Historic Environment Scotland

Jim Johnson

Keppie Design

LDN Architects

LoveMilton

MAKAR

NB Planning

Richard Atkins Chartered Architect

Robin Baker Architects

Simon Winstanley Architects

Simpson and Brown Architects

Smith Scott Mullan Associates

The National Trust for Scotland

SEDA Design Guides

Between 2005 and 2008 the Scottish Ecological Design Association commissioned three design guides funded by the Scottish Government. These guides dealt in turn with designing and detailing for deconstruction, airtightness and toxic chemical reduction in buildings.

The guides are aimed at mainstream commercial construction and should be useful for Architects, Developers, Contractors and others within the Construction Industry who wish to reduce the environmental damage associated with their projects. Each guide covers five typical construction types, each of which was carefully assessed by Cost Consultants and Insurability Assessors.

The guides on the following pages are available to download for free by following the links at SEDA's website: www.seda.uk.net

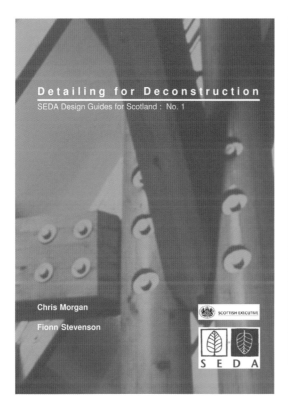

Detailing for Deconstruction

SEDA Design Guides for Scotland : No. 1

Chris Morgan

Fionn Stevenson

SCOTTISH EXECUTIVE

S E D A

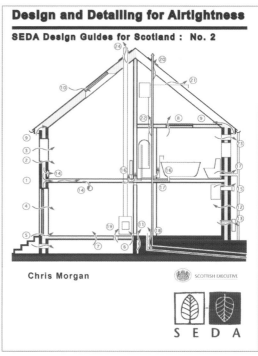

Design and Detailling for Airtightness

SEDA Design Guides for Scotland : No. 2

Chris Morgan

SCOTTISH EXECUTIVE

S E D A

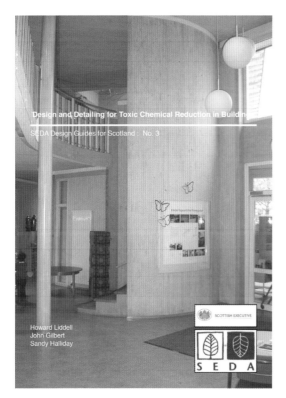

Design and Detailling for Toxic Chemical Reduction in Buildin

SEDA Design Guides for Scotland : No. 3

Howard Liddell
John Gilbert
Sandy Halliday

SCOTTISH EXECUTIVE

S E D A